WHAT OUR STUDENTS ARE SAYING:

Here are some responses from students who have taken the in-person version of *The Art and Craft of Writing*:

"The course is a treasure trove of practical, positive advice you can use immediately to improve your WIP or solidify your ideas for a new project." Marina Fontaine, author of *Chasing Freedom*.

"I took L. Jagi Lamplighter Wright's "Guinea Pig" writing class in November of 2018 and it definitely upped my game. Since "graduating" her course, I've sold over 30 short stories and 2 novellas (as of February 2021). Thanks, Jagi." —James Pyles, author of multiple published short stories.

"I especially liked how you simply laid out ideas about story and characters, which instantly made me go, 'Oh, yeah! I've seen that before!'... I felt that these were techniques that would have taken me ages to work out on my own, and seeing them simply stated has seriously helped me as a writer."—Billy Charlton, teen student.

THE ART AND CRAFT OF WRITING

L. JAGI LAMPLIGHTER

WISECRAFT

Wisecraft Publishing

Copyright © 2020 by L. Jagi Lamplighter

All rights reserved. No part of the content of this book may be reproduced, distributed, or transmitted in any form or by any means, or stored in a database retrieval system, or copied by any technology yet to be developed without the prior written permission of the author. You may not circulate this book in any format.

ISBN: 978-1-953739-04-9

To Donald Maass and Margie Lawson,
Whose investigation into our art and craft inspired mine.

And to Jim Frenkel,
who taught me so much.
Thank you.

HOW BEST TO USE THIS BOOK

This is a book on how to write. Specifically, it is a book on how to bring your current writing to the next level. How to make what you do better.

As a Book

The Art and Craft of Writing can be read through as a book.

As a Workbook

More will be accomplished if you pause to do the exercises. It is in striving to accomplish the assignments that we are often forced to stretch our understanding. This leads to us learning more than if we did not attempt this.

As a Self-Taught Class

Best of all, however, is if you tackle this program with a friend.

The Art and Craft of Writing works best when two or three authors* work together.

Find two or three writer friends and form Working Partners. Read the chapters, do the exercises, and then swap your results with your Working Partner. The Working Partners then review each other's work.

Having someone with whom to share work has several benefits. It encourages students to complete the assignments. It helps students assess whether they correctly understood the assignments. It is also makes it easier to stay focused and remember to complete the next chapter in a timely manner.

It is much easier to motivate ourselves to write if you know someone else is waiting to see what you have accomplished.

Students of online *The Art and Craft of Writing* classes have discovered that an ideal schedule to avoid burnout is to do two to four chapters, one per week, and then take a break of a few weeks before tackling the next two to four chapters. But whatever you and your Working Partner find comfortable will work.

*If there are four or more of you, it is best to divide into subgroups of two or three. That way no one is overburdened by having to read too many other people's assignments.

As an Accompaniment for *The Art and Craft of Writing* Video Lessons

All of the above three methods can be done in accompaniment with the video lessons. The material in the book and video is very similar, though the book contains a small amount of additional material.

In Conclusion

Whatever method you choose, it is our hope that this book will bring you both enjoyment and increased understanding of both the art and the craft of your chosen trade.

CONTENTS

Words on a Page	13
Part One: The Craft of Writing The Essential Elements	17
Chapter 1: The Trick	19
Chapter 2: Breathing Life into Your Characters	27
Chapter 3: Descriptions That Grip	41
Chapter 4: Two Strings	53
Chapter 5: To Anticipate or Not to Anticipate?	63
Chapter 6: The Ultimate Secret	73
Part Two: The Craft of Writing Refining the Craft	85
Chapter 7: Engaging Openings	87
Chapter 8: Plot We've Got...	105
Chapter 9: Infodumps Begone!	115
Chapter 10: Wow, That Was Satisfying!	127
Part Three: The Art of Writing	139
Chapter 11: Heart and Soul	141
Chapter 12: Interior Dialogue	153
Chapter 13: Payload Moments	161
Chapter 14: The Trouble with Tropes	171
Final Word: Writing Tips	189
Resources	193
Acknowledgments	195

WORDS ON A PAGE

All writing is just words on a page.

What does this mean, and why does it matter to us? To answer that question, I must tell you a bit of a story.

When I was young, I was in awe of the ability of good authors to transport us to an entirely different life. Reading the greats was glorious but also occasionally intimidating. A good book can make us sympathize first with a frightened rabbit and then with a hungry fox. They call upon us to "burn with the bliss and suffer the sorrow of all mankind.*"

I loved what I read, but I despaired that I could ever write anything half so wonderful. I feared I would never figure out the mystery of how my favorite authors conveyed so much.

Then one day, it struck me.

Books were just words on a page.

Nothing more.

If an author could convey something within the pages of his book, it had to have been accomplished by the use of specific, individual words.

If I could figure out which words produced which effects, I could learn to do the same.

I remember one of the first times I figured out how to indicate an emotion indirectly. I was quite proud of myself. However, it led to an unexpectedly funny conversation with a dear family member who had some very odd beliefs, including that he had some sort of extra sensory perception.

My family member: *I perceive here that your main character is angry.*

Me, delighted: *Yes! I went out of my way to slip that in. So glad it worked.*

My family member: *No. I'm not talking about what you wrote. I am telling you that I am discerning that your character is secretly bitter about what is going on.*

Me: *Yes, I put that in, on purpose.*

My family member: *No, I am telling you that I am picking this up psychically.*

I didn't win that argument, but I had successfully taken my first small steps towards using words to capture the magic that is the story.

In the lessons within this book, we will consider words upon a page. We will look at how to make them work for us instead of against us, at what kind of words we need to put down to get the effects we desire to achieve.

Books are enchanting. They are like a draught of strong wine. A good story sweeps us off our feet and caries us to true love, to far off places, to Narnia or Barsoom. As writers of stories, we can reach others, lift them out of sorrow, sometimes even sway the course of lives, or nations.

All of us yearn to write, including you, dear reader, or you would not be reading this. We long to bring to vivid life those stories that burn deep within our hearts. We wish not only to see them given life but also to share them and, perhaps, to touch the heart of another.

Books may just be words on a page, *but look what we can make those words do!*

* -- "*Burn with the bliss and suffer the sorrow of all mankind*"— my father's favorite line from the Hindu religious epic, *Bhagavad Gita*.

Welcome to The Art and Craft of Writing

PART ONE: THE CRAFT OF WRITING THE ESSENTIAL ELEMENTS

CHAPTER 1: THE TRICK

The Trick: *If you want a scene to culminate in a particular emotional reaction, start the scene with the opposite emotion.*

Anticipation

When Disney started his animation studio, he and his artists had to invent the tools of the animation trade. No one had ever done it before. One problem they ran into was that viewers had trouble telling what the figures on the screen were doing. Disney solved this with an animation principle his artists called *anticipation*. In anticipation, as the concept was developed by the Disney studio, a character leans left to run right. He bends down to jump up. He pulls his arm back to throw a ball forward. This allowed for an exaggerated motion that helped the viewer track the action the character was performing.

The same is true with The Trick—only, in writing, the actions are all emotional.

In some ways, The Trick is the secret to all writing, the thing that makes a story work. It could be summed up as:

establishing an expectation followed by something other than the expected outcome.

Of all writing techniques, The Trick is the easiest to do. You just decide where you want the story to go, and then you indicate—through dialogue, character thought, or narration—that the opposite is coming.

If you want to have a happy incident, you first make your character glum.

If you want something bad to happen, you first make him unexpectedly confident.

It is that simple, and it is tremendously effective. You have to remember to use it.

That is all.

How best to use it, of course, gets more difficult. If you are too blatant about your reversals, the audience will not be taken in. Some books and shows are so obvious that every time someone is happy, the audience winces, certain that something bad is around the corner. Being that obvious undercuts the effect. The reader is put on alert rather than lulled into a false sense of security.

So, the more subtly you can apply The Trick, the more effective your scene. But you would be amazed at how blatant you can be and still have it work. Some of the best-selling authors today are quite obvious in their use of the Trick, and yet people read their books with great eagerness.

Rebecca's Ups and Downs

An excellent primer for understanding The Trick is the book *Rebecca* by Daphne du Maurier. In this book, the plot reverses on a regular basis. If the main character thinks something good is coming, something bad happens. If she expects the worst, it turns out well. The whole book is the juxtaposition between a young woman's fantasies and the contrasting reality that ensues.

If you think you understand the principle of The Trick so far, excellent. If not, take a look at *Rebecca*, read a few scenes. You will soon see how it is accomplished.

Other good examples? Harry Potter. Which is more surprising, more interesting: the world is saved by a rich, popular boy? Or an unwanted boy who lives under the stairs saves the world?

The Hobbit: which is more surprising: a great hero defeats the Dark Lord? Or an ordinary, short, country hobbit defeats the Dark Lord?

Strider is a really great example. He appears all dark and sinister when the Hobbits first come upon him in Bree. No one expected a cloaked figure sitting in the dark in an inn—the epitome of a robber or bad character—to be the hidden king! (He is such a good example that Tolkien even wrote a poem about it.)

The Trick Gets Tricky

Where the Trick gets, well, tricky is when there is more than one expected outcome, either one of which will not surprise anyone. The author is then called upon to do some clever thinking and find a third option that will surprise and delight. Sometimes, this takes time and creativity, but it is usually worth the effort.

I ran into this problem in my *Prospero's Children* series. *Prospero's Children*, for those who have not read it, is a modern fantasy sequel to Shakespeare's *Tempest*. The plot starts out with the main character, Miranda, daughter of the Dread Magician Prospero, believing that everything is fine. Then, aspersions are cast upon her father. A long adventure ensues. After a while, either obvious outcome "Prospero is innocent of the charges against him" or "Prospero is guilty" no longer seems that interesting.

Either way, there is no Trick.

(The innocent option leaves the reader thinking: "Well, why did I go through reading all that just to get back where I started?" The guilty option seems too pat: "Prospero was accused of X and Y in Book One and by Book Three, we find out X and Y are true. So? You told us that two books ago.")

Solving this problem, coming up with an ending that did not disappoint, took quite some effort (and an idea on the philosophy of storytelling that I borrowed from J. R. R. Tolkien.) I had to find an option that followed from what had been established but that reversed what was expected while not being not too easily anticipated. Ultimately, it was, again, a matter of the Trick.

But How Does It Actually Work?

How exactly does one use The Trick? Let me use an example from real life.

A man's house was foreclosed on by Bank of America. It was a condo, really, but it was his home. It was a very sad thing because he had been up on his payments; however, there had been a misunderstanding. Some years earlier, he had lost his job. During his jobless period, he had arranged payment plan with the bank, where he was paying a portion of the monthly amount.

This man, we will call him Thadeus, was a hard worker. When he got a new job, he approached Bank of America and offered to return to the full payment. The person on the phone told him to stick to the current payment plan.

Fast forward a few years, Thadeus gets a sudden call

from Bank of America. They say: Pay up the many thousand dollars you are now behind, immediately. Obviously, he did not have this on hand. He lost his home.

Time went by. There was a class-action suit against the bank. Thadeus participated and was part of a winning settlement.

A few days ago, the check arrived. He sat with it in his hand for almost half an hour, praying and terrified, before he opened it. You see, he knew that while some people had gotten as much as $3000 from the settlement, many had only received $300. He did not know if he could bear it if his check contained only $300.

Finally, he ripped open the envelope. It contained a check for *$6000!*

What a relief!

He paid some bills, called his friends, and celebrated! And we, the readers, celebrate with him!

Pause a moment. Think of how that makes you feel. Okay. Ready? Let's go on.

Now, there's another part of this story. Thadeus worked in an office, but he had always wanted to do more. When he graduated from college, he wanted to serve in the army or as a police officer. He wanted to do a job that mattered. He applied to many places. Each time, he was turned down due to ill health.

That was nearly twenty years ago. His health improved. Recently, he discovered that he might qualify to become a firefighter. This is the kind of work he could excel at—active work helping people with truly important things.

To make this change work, it would help a great deal if he could take some paramedic classes. This will be difficult for him, of course, because taking classes while working is always a strain.

When word first came about the B of A settlement, he looked online to find out how much he might be getting. The top payment for someone in his category was $125,000!

Even though he knew this was probably an exaggeration, Thadeus spent an evening daydreaming of what he might do if he received the entire $125,000. He could quit his job, pay off his debts, and take the classes! He could be free of his current life entirely! He could be the man he wished to be.

Eventually, he discovered that this was not the amount people in his position would receive—and the fears of receiving only $300 began.

Now, think of how different the story above would have felt if it had read: He held the envelope, expecting, hoping, that it would contain $125,000. All his hopes for the future, all his dreams, lay in this one check. He ripped the envelope open.

Instead of a miraculous triumph, that same exact $6000 now feels like a crushing defeat.

That's *the Trick*.

Exercise: The Trick

Try the trick!

Pick a scene—it can be a short or long—and perform The Trick.

Have the character start out in one mood/emotion and

end up in an opposite or contrasting emotional position by the end of the scene.

If you don't have a scene, make one up. It can be very short. Just show a character having one emotional reaction and ending up in an opposing emotional state.

CHAPTER 2: BREATHING LIFE INTO YOUR CHARACTERS

Living Characters: *To make a character come to life, give him two conflicting qualities and/or goals.*

Characters are the heart and soul of your story.

They are how the reader connects to the events of your plot. If you want your readers to "burn with the bliss and suffer the sorrow" of your story, you need to present them with characters who engage their sympathy, their love, their hatred.

Characters who come alive.

The first thing you need to know when you sit down to write is: *who is the main character?*

The answer to this is: *The main character is the one who does the thing.*

Whoever performs the main action, makes the main thing happen, commits the pivotal act—that is who your story is about.

If this isn't who you are writing about, you must either change the action of the story so that it accomplished by your main character (or characters) or rewrite—making the person who does perform the pivotal act the star of the story.

Once you have your main characters, how do you bring them and your secondary characters to life?

The Secret Is in the Shading

Imagine that you and I are standing in front of an easel upon which an artist has drawn a circle. It's just a circle. We tilt our head left and right, but there's nothing else there.

One line. Round.

Flat.

Then, the artist comes forward. He squints slightly to the left, as if envisioning the light source. Then he picks up his charcoal pencil and adds shading, a darker bit around the curve, a lighter bit a little farther up and down.

And, *voila!* Suddenly, our circle has become a sphere, a ball fairly bouncing off the page.

Shading is a marvelous thing, a simple trick. Once you know how to do it, your pictures need never look flat again.

Ah, you say, sighing, as you look at the curve of the charcoal beach ball, if only it were that simple to make three-dimensional characters.

The good news is: *It is.*

So, how is it done? Like with art, it is easy to explain but takes practice to accomplish. The principle, however, is simple.

What transforms a circle into a ball is the contrast between the whiteness of the paper and the darkness of the shading. Put simply: Contrast is what makes drawings 3-D. To make a character leap off the page, the same thing is needed—contrast.

The master of understanding this is New York literary agent Donald Maass. We will talk more about Maass below.

Character Dimensions

Characters come in three types: one-dimensional, two-dimensional, and three-dimensional.

One-dimensional characters act and talk. They aren't really different from each other.

Two-dimensional characters have specific identifying characteristics and are clearly identifiable as these characters, but they never act outside these limits. They can be really good characters, but they are limited. (Think of the Peanuts comic strip. Charlie Brown is a loveable character, but he's never going to hit the ball.)

Three-dimensional characters have an independent life of their own. They seem to move and breathe.

To continue with our drawing metaphor:

1D – stick figure
2D – black and white line drawing
3D – sketch with shading and even color

Does Dimension Matter?

Why is character dimension important?

The more dimensions a character has, the more unexpectedly the character can act and still be clearly within the scope of what has been established for that character. Such a character is more interesting to read about. This makes the whole work seem more real to the reader.

Imagine you are writing a scene and your main character is a baker.

. . .

One-Dimensional Characters: A one dimensional baker just says lines. The fact that he is a baker never really comes up.

Two-Dimensional Characters: A 2-D baker looks at everything from a baker's point of view. He mentions baker's dozens and talks about how much bread you need to feed people or how hot you can make an oven, etc. He sees the world through baker's eyes.

This is refreshing to readers, as they are not bakers and don't know how a baker sees things, but it can become overly predictable.

Some of the most beloved characters in the world are two-dimensional. Many cartoon characters fall into this category—characters, such as the beloved *Peanuts* mentioned above, who always do the same thing. Such characters can be iconic and endearing, but they never change.

They can be great for short works and for fast moving thrillers or mysteries, any story where the internal world of the character is secondary to the action; however, it would be hard to carry a more reflective novel with such a character, as novel readers expect their characters to alter and change with the events.

Three-Dimensional Characters: Imagine your baker is also a father. When he goes into a scene, he can react as a baker, or as a father.

This immediately allows for his reactions to be a bit more unexpected.

Now imagine he is also a Christian, and he also plays the guitar. Now you have four different in character reactions you could have when he arrives in a scene, he could make a comment that reflects baking, fatherhood, Christianity, or music. Suddenly, he literally has a number of different dimensions to his personality.

Adding Shading that is Contrast

How do we do this? How do we decide what additional qualities to add to our characters in order to catapult them into the third dimension? Luckily for us, someone has cracked that case, and the secret is out!

One of the best books on writing fiction is Donald Maass's *Writing the Breakout Novel* and its associated *Writing the Breakout Novel Workbook*. Maass is a New York agent who has read thousands of submitted manuscripts and seen which ones went on to sell well. One day, he became curious about whether there was a significant difference between the average book and the novels that broke out. So, he set out to discover the answer.

Breakout here is defined as: sold many more than expected. These breakout novels were either ones that the publisher did not put much attention into, and yet the book did really well; or a book by an author who had normally sold at one level who suddenly leapt to a higher level—for instance, an author whose books regularly sell 5,000 copies, suddenly sells 20,000 copies.

Maass decided to investigate the matter by reading one hundred breakout novels. His discover? They *were* different. They *were* better. He then set out to pinpoint what made these books different, and he shared his analysis with us in *Writing the Breakout Novel*.

In my humble opinion, Maass's book is the best and most useful work on writing out there. The market portion of the book is out of date, but the writing advice is spot on.

He analyses what all these stories have in common and lays out the points one at a time. We shall discuss a couple of his points in this book. Right now, let us look at his insight into the nature of character.

Maass's book and his workbook are both excellent, but he has an exercise on page 64 of the *Workbook* that is excellent for helping authors to add three-dimensionality to characters. In short:

A) *Take a character.*

Write down that character's main quality.

Write down an opposite quality.

Write a paragraph or short scene where the character demonstrates the opposing quality.

(Ex: A happy character shows a moment of fear or sorrow. A grumpy character cheers up briefly. Etc.)

B) *Take the same character.*

Write down that character's main goal

Write down an opposing goal

Write a paragraph or short scene showing how these two goals are pulling your character in two directions.

So how does this work?

The key to developing three-dimensional characters is giving them contrasting qualities or goals. If your character is a curmudgeon, have a scene where you show his sweet side. If she is forever happy, show a touch of bitterness under the surface. If he is glum, show the moment when he temporarily forgets his glumness and is transported. If she is efficient, show the area where she just loses it, or maybe she's clumsy.

The same applies for the second part of Maass's exercise, which is to write down your character's goal and then give the character a conflicting goal. Let the character that longs to wander also love his garden at home. The goal of travel and the goal of being at home to tend your garden are opposites and can't both be accomplished at the same time; this gives the character a natural conflict.

Again, any character who has two conflicting goals—two things they want to do that are in some way mutually exclusive—becomes more dynamic.

Opposing vs. Conflicting:

Maass's exercise calls for "opposite" traits, but time and experience has led me to amend that to "conflicting." Sometimes, the actual opposite trait won't work for a specific character, but a conflicting quality will accomplish the same purpose.

What, you might ask, do I mean by conflicting qualities?

Conflicting qualities are qualities that normally don't go together: graceful and grumpy. Frightened and proud. Awkward, yet confident. Maybe your nice guy really isn't mean—so "opposing" qualities will not work—but he could be glum, or despondent, or grumpy, or wistful. These conflicting traits achieve the desired effect of broadening the character's scope and making him more than just the stock nice guy.

Or imagine we have a character whose magic power requires that he *always tells the truth*. The opposite would be *lie*. But lying might dramatically be out of character for this particular person, or maybe he is actually incapable of lying. Again, the opposing quality is not useful for the story. Contrasting qualities, however, can still help this character spring to life. Perhaps, he desires not to hurt another character's feelings. The goal *tell the truth* and the goal *spare his feel-*

ings are not opposites, but they are contrasting. A scene where the character deals with these two issues could be quite interesting, depending on what tack the character takes. Or perhaps he tells the truth, but he occasionally blurts out too much. His honesty is now countered by his rudeness.

Why does this work?

As we established above, two-dimensional characters always act the same way. They are recognizable. They can even be loveable—as a flat drawing with no shading can still be quite appealing—but something is lacking.

2-D characters are always cheerful or always disapproving. That is what makes them stock characters, characters for whom we can predict exactly what their reaction would be. In *Peanuts,* for instance, when likable klutz Charley Brown goes to kick the football, Lucy will always move the ball at the last minute.

Add another dimension, however, and the character's actions can become unexpected without leaving the realm of what has been established about the character. To return to our example from above, if, in a scene where bakers are talking together, our baker-father-Christian-guitarist character suddenly runs to stop a small child from sticking his hand into a hot oven, because his fatherly instincts are kicking in, it can be unexpected—but not out of character because the reader already knows that the character is also a father. If he whips out his guitar and sings a pretty ditty about the life of a baker, soothing an argument that is about to explode among his fellows, that, too, is unexpected and yet, we already know that he plays the guitar. Being able to respond in a way that is unexpected, but not out of character, is what gives characters that lifelike quality that we call three-dimensional.

Real people are quirky; they are multifaceted. Even people who are stuck in their ways occasionally have their moments where they rise above their limited behaviors to something more. Imitating this in our writing is what brings a character to life.

Frankly, My Dear, I Don't Give a...

An example that comes to mind is Rhett Butler in *Gone with the Wind*. When it becomes clear that the South is losing, the previously-casual rascal, who has taken nothing seriously up until this point, suddenly decides to join the army. This is so different from his normal way of behaving —from his two-dimensional front as a carefree blockade runner—that it is a shocking surprise.

No one expects the privateer who cares only for his own profit to show a sense of loyalty and responsibility. Those qualities conflict with everything we have seen of him thus far.

And yet, the character is so skillfully drawn that the reader does not think, *"Oh, come on, he would never do that. This is ridiculous. I'm not reading this tripe."* Instead, the reader feels as if the true Rhett is suddenly coming to the foreground.

Why? Because we know that the other string to his "scofflaw rascal present" is his "Southern gentleman past." Under pressure, it is these secondary qualities, his sense of honor, his sense of loyalty—his pre-established but secondary Southern gentleman upbringing—that come to the fore.

The action is surprising and yet understandable.

And that is what we want in our characters. We want them to surprise our readers and yet make them go, *"Oh, of course!"* It is that kind of depth that makes characters come alive.

When the artist adds shading to his circle, it tricks the eye so that we think an extra dimension is present. An expert artist can make that beach ball bounce right off the page. But even an amateur can quickly learn to use shading to give a sense of curve and depth to his circle.

Similarly, an expert writer can bring characters to life at the touch of a keystroke. But by applying the simple trick of demonstrating unexpected contrasting qualities, even new writers can give their characters depth and life.

Who Would Run the World?

When I was writing my *Prospero's Children* series, I tried this exercise myself for the first time. I was impressed with how quickly it breathed life into my secondary characters and villains. I ended up putting every scene that I produced using this exercise into the final novel. The paragraphs improved the story—made each character to whom I applied it more interesting, more dynamic.

In the trilogy, Prospero has gone missing. In order to rescue him, the main character, Miranda, must round up the other children he has sired in the several hundred years since the events recorded in Shakespeare's *Tempest*. These additional brothers and sisters were prime fodder for Maass's character-expanding exercise.

One character I tackled was Miranda's blind brother, Cornelius. Each Prospero offspring has a vice with which he or she struggled. Cornelius's is ambition. He runs the Illuminati and is a power-behind-the-throne type.

So, when I set out to do Maass's exercise for Cornelius, I asked myself: What is the opposite of *wanting to secretly be in charge of everything?*

What I came up with was: *the desire to retire.* Here is the scene I wrote in response to Maass's exercise. The *Prospero's Children* trilogy is written in a first-person noir style, so "I" refers to Miranda. This scene was ultimately added to *Prospero In Hell*, the second volume of the trilogy.

"...And you?" I asked, "What would you do, if you could do anything?"

"Retire to the Riviera, or maybe an island like Father's," Cornelius replied, cutting his fish.

"Retire?"

"Is that so very strange?" Cornelius smiled faintly. He leaned back. "Mortals get to retire. Their usefulness comes to an end, and they are rewarded for their toil with a period of leisure. Have you ever had a period of leisure, Sister? I know I haven't. I so envy Father's recent retirement."

"What would you do if you retired?" I asked.

"Sit on the beach, feel the sun on my face, and listen to music. At night, I would hire my own string quartet to play my favorite pieces exactly as I like them."

I blinked. "That...would be nice. Can't you try it?"

Returning to cutting his fish, Cornelius snorted. "If I retired, who would run the world?"

One exercise, a few lines, and Cornelius suddenly had a great deal more personality than he had exhibited previously. I was able to build on his conflicting goals toward the end of the series to develop his character even more. Then I went on and applied the same principle to half a dozen other characters, including all four of the villains.

Exercise A: Qualities

Pick a character and try Maas's first exercise:

A) *Take a character.*
Write down that character's main quality.
Write down a contrasting quality.
Write a paragraph or short scene where the character demonstrates the contrasting quality.

Exercise B: Goals

When you are done, take a character—the same one or a different one, and try the second exercise:

B) *Take the same character.*
Write down that character's main goal.
Write down a contrasting goal.
Write a paragraph or short scene showing how these two goals are pulling your character in two directions.

Try two or three characters—using A or B as seems to best fit that character. No need to use them both unless you are really on a roll.

Bonus Exercise: Through Another's Eyes

Readers love seeing characters through the eyes of other characters. If done well, it gives them an interesting glimpse of the known characters from the point of view of someone who sees the characters differently than the characters see themselves. What does your main character look like to his mother? His teacher? His rival? Someone who barely knows him?

Pick two characters. Ask yourself some of these questions:

What does character B know about character A?

Has B heard false rumors about A? Are they good or bad?

Is B unaware of something major about A?

Does B dislike something about A that previously has been shown in a positive light?

Is B impressed with some quality about A that the reader may have overlooked?

Write a paragraph describing character A through the eyes of character B.

CHAPTER 3: DESCRIPTIONS THAT GRIP

Descriptions That Grip: *Add two to five senses to every description.*

The Blank White Room

Where does your story take place? In a blank white room? Because blank whiteness is going to be what the reader sees if you don't fill in a location.

In contemporary stories—particularly thrillers—it is common to use very little description. This is because the book takes place in an environment the reader knows. "A hotel room" or "the local convenience store" is all that is needed to convey an entire setting. Any more than this might take away from the non-stop flow of the action.

This method only works, however, if your story is grounded in the familiar. If your story takes place in a historical, science fiction, or fantasy setting, it is up to you to set the stage.

To this end, we shall discuss two description techniques

that can help draw your reader into the richness that is the alternate reality you wish to convey.

Description Technique 1: Senses

When I started writing, I used to swap pages I had finished that week with two writer friends. We would read each other's work and send back comments. My friend's comments were almost universally the same. They constantly complained that I had not included any sense impression except for sight.

"What does it sound like?" They would ask. "What does it smell like?"

At first, I added additional sense impressions only at their urging. With time, I began to remember to do it myself—but it was an artificial process. I had to go back after my first draft and deliberately add them. Now, the majority of the time, I remember as I am writing the scene the first time.

You might ask: Why? What's the big deal about sound and smell, and maybe taste or feel?

The answer: The more vivid the description, the more real the experience of reading about it feels.

Imagine you had someone in a virtual reality suit, and you wanted to convince them that your program was the real world—not to delude them, to entertain. No matter how realistic your visuals, if they heard and smelled their living room—the old sock their son left by the rocking chair, the odor from where their daughter had not properly cleaned up after the dog, the sound of their neighbors arguing—they would never be entirely swept away by your vivid waterfalls and grand vistas.

But what if you could make them hear the roar of the water and smell the resin of the newly-broken pine? What if they could feel the cool breeze and could taste the icy, mineral-laden water? Wouldn't that go much further toward convincing them that your scenario was real?

When it comes right down to it, how do we tell where we are? By the sights, sounds, tastes, smells, and feel of things. Those are the methods we use to collect information. If those senses were fooled, we would come to the conclusion that we were somewhere else.

Our real senses are the most convincing, of course, but we have a second pair of senses, too—our imaginary senses. We can imagine seeing the warm brown walls of our favorite coffee shop; hearing the percolating liquids; smelling the roasted coffee; tasting the hot sweet drink (after six pumps of syrup have been added); and feeling the heat of the cup between our hands.

With enough imaginative pointers, we can get a vivid mental image.

Which brings us back to writing. Basically, we writers yearn to enchant our readers—to draw them away from their actual life—until the life on the page seems as vivid as reality. Or more so. The more successful we are, the more readers forget their surroundings and are drawn into the story—making it more likely that they will keep on reading...

...and that they will enjoy the experience.

But how do we actually do it?

You picture a scene in your head, searching through your imagination and memory for what such a place and time might look, sound, smell, taste, and feel like. Then you add these specifics to your description. Not only does this make the experience more vivid for the reader, but it also forces the author to think about the scene in more detail.

Often, when pausing to figure out what a character

might be hearing or smelling, authors discover aspects of the scenario that they had not considered. Maybe, they had forgotten to take into consideration the loudness of the waterfall or how cold a mountain top would be in late November. Adding accurate details to the scene increases its reality in the mind of the readers.

Sense impressions can be added in two ways: directly or indirectly. When added directly, the sentence is just about the sense—*the seat was hot. The air smelled like peppermint.* When added indirectly, the sense is mentioned as part of the ongoing narrative—*he reached for the shovel, yanking his hand back from the icy cold metal. A hint of peppermint mingled with the smoky air.*

Each of the senses is important. Let's take a look at each one.

Sight

For *sight*, you want to pick objects to describe that convey the mood of the surroundings. If possible, it is useful to do so in order: left to right, or up to down—the way a camera would pan over the scene—because, really, isn't the camera just copying what our eyes naturally do when we move our head?

"He had red hair, a green shirt, and long black boots" is easier to picture than "He had long black boots, red hair, and a green shirt."

Panning in this way is not always possible. Sometimes, for emphasis purpose, one needs to end a description in the middle, but it is a useful tip where applicable.

Hearing

Hearing is the easiest second sense to add, because if there is nothing interesting to hear up close, there is always an opportunity for something farther away. Up close, the computer hums, and the kitten is snoring. Farther away is the buzz of the heater. Beyond that, outdoors, a bird caws. Occasionally, a louder roar shakes the house as a plane departs a nearby airport. Thus, the author has a choice. Include the sound of something up close, to add vividness to the surroundings, or mention a far away noise, something that reminds the reader of the larger world beyond your characters.

Smell

The third easiest is *smell*. Scents are both simple and difficult. Sometimes, there really isn't much to interest the nose. I can't smell anything interesting at the moment here at my desk. Even when I stuck my nose in the wrapper of a mint candy left on the table, most of the minty goodness had already escaped.

However, when smells are present, they can be overpowering—especially bad smells. Adding the odor of dank laundry or a hint of pine-scented cleaner can immediately bring a crisp vividness to an otherwise lagging description.

Feeling

Feelings come in two kinds: what objects feel like and what your body feels. From the point of view of the writer evoking the readers' senses, these can be two different experiences. If one writes, *"Colleen shivered from the bite of the icy breeze,"* it evokes a different mental experience from, *"The table had not been sanded. The wood was rough and splintery."*

The first description tells us what Colleen's body experiences. These types of descriptions include temperature and other sensations that affect our bodies directly. Is the room hot or cold—humidity, weather conditions? Is the wind buffeting face and hair? Pain could be included in this category, depending on how the author described it. The second tells us about the physical properties of objects. Are they smooth or rough? Spongy or unyielding? Sticky or dry?

Both of these kinds of descriptions are valuable in writing. You can even put them in the same paragraph. From a descriptive writing point of view, they can almost be used as two different senses.

Taste

Finally, *taste*. Frankly, it is difficult to find places to use taste in most scenes—unless your hero is a dog or a snake who can afford to go around licking ordinary objects. If the opportunity arises, however, seize it! Obviously, scenes involving food are great places to mention that something tastes sweet or salty or spicy or like warm chocolate or barbequed chicken or a particularly juicy steak smothered in mint and rosemary. Bad tastes can also be used to heighten the unpleasantness of a less-than-ideal situation.

How Much Spice?

Experience suggests that adding all five sense impressions to every scene makes descriptions top-heavy. So how many senses should be added?

Two is a good start. If you can find a place in a descriptive paragraph to include three sense impressions, the scenario often feels more vivid without being overly-bogged down by too much description. More than three requires a significant commitment to description, more than many authors find comfortable, though occasionally an opportunity arises to include four or five while still keeping the flow of the narrative.

There is no hard and fast rule. Sometimes, just one will do; other times, more than three will work. But two to three different kinds of sense is a good start. The best thing is to try it and see what works with your story's mood and style.

Where, oh, Where?

The question arises: Where should these descriptions of sense impressions go?

Short answer: Anywhere you like.

Longer answer: In addition to putting descriptions where it feels needed, it is often wise to include at least a short description at the beginning of a new scene or location. Your readers have just arrived in a new blank white room. Paint them a picture of the place you want them to be.

If your main character has just walked into a school, pause a moment to mention the bright teal lockers, the sound of students laughing, the hint of cleaning products in the humid air. If she has stepped onto a sailboat for the first time, mention the salty scent of the sea, the creak of the ropes, the cry of gulls, possibly the sun beating down upon her head or maybe the wind blowing her bonnet. If he is spelunking in a cave, mention the wet rock, the earthen odor, the drop-drip of water somewhere in the dark, cavernous space.

Notice how just a few sense impressions help make the location more vivid in the reader's imagination. Definitely worth the time it takes to add them.

A useful side-effect for a writer is that stopping to think about sense impressions makes the author more aware of the entire scenario. I probably would never have noticed that I can feel the weave of my sweater or hear both the regular whir of my heater and the gentle *mrrr* of a cat had I not paused to pay attention.

What can you hear?

What is your body feeling right now?

When we sit down and stretch our imaginations, piecing together what a distant time and place might sound and smell like, our whole story becomes crisper in our minds—and, thus, through our words, in the minds of our readers.

Description Technique 2: Emotions

Descriptions are also wonderful vehicles for expressing emotion. Is the character joyful or heartbroken, angry or at peace? These are things that you can hint at when writing a description. Let's take a look:

Happy

The sky was bright and blue. The young woman jumped through the puddles with the enthusiasm of a child playing hopscotch. Water splashed everywhere. The wet droplets felt cool upon her cheek.

Heartbroken

The sky was gray and overcast. A faint rumble of thunder sounded in the distance. The young woman moved as if in a dream, sloshing through the puddles. Her sopping-wet shoes dragged heavily upon her feet.

Angry
Despite the oppressive heat, the young woman stomped from puddle to puddle, slamming her foot down as if to eradicate each one from existence.

At Peace
Overhead, the sky was a perfect collage of clouds and blue. A robin called, and, somewhere in the distance, a lawn mower hummed. The young woman strolled down a path freckled with puddles, gently stepping over them as she went.

In each version, a young woman travels by some puddles, but the weather and the young woman's interaction with the puddles change, depending on her mood.

This example included a young woman doing the acting, but a similar effect can be achieved without any person present at all. *The clouds hung low over the countryside like a smothering blanket* gives a different impression of the same late afternoon landscape than: *Clouds cloaked the world in mystery.*

One thing to keep in mind is that weather does not have to match the character's mood. The sun can shine on a sad character, who might be resentful of the cheery day, or rain can fall on a happy one, who perhaps rejoices, dancing among the raindrops. In each case, the goal is to pick images that will help convey to the reader the entire experience, so that they come as close as possible to living your story.

Exercise A:

Pick a spot—it can be in your house, in the woods, at a local coffee shop. If you have the time, use this exercise as a chance to go to some spot you might not normally visit.

Sit comfortably and jot down everything around you. Note sensations, smells, sounds, what you see, heat and cold.

Write down this list of observations. Try to note a minimum of ten. For instance:

Trees
Ferns
River running slowly, leaves swirling on the surface
Clouds blue
Lawnmower in the distance
Smell of loam
Oak bark
Small silvery fish in river
Ground damp
Boulder with flakes of mica.
Or
Beige rug
Large desk designed for a corner
Papers strewn across desk
Flashlight seated beside computer monitor
Phone
Bobblehead of Castiel
Paper flowers
Sound of rain pelting porch from clogged gutters
Smell of mint tea
White mouse on a mouse pad showing a book cover.

Exercise B: Write a description using these elements:

Exercise C:
Now look around and ask yourself several of these questions, taking notes as needed to answer them:
What if it were night—what would you notice?
What if it were raining—how would it look different? (or, if it is raining, what if it were sunny?)
What if you were scared and hiding in this spot?
What if you were really happy?
What if you were sad or gloomy?
What if this was a mystery—what objects might you note?

Then write two or more descriptions of the spot you picked: one simple description, including at least two or three senses, and at least one additional description using prompts from above (i.e, describe the same place as if it were night, or you were hiding, or you were sad, etc.)

Exercise D:
Pick a place in your work in progress and do the same exercise for that imaginary spot: Imagine you were there, write a list of what you would see, hear, feel, smell, etc.. Then write a description of that place.
Write a second version of the imaginary spot adjusting for the time of day, weather, or mood of the character, etc.

Do this as many times as you like, picking appropriate places in your manuscript.

Bonus Exercise:

Specific details can add to the vividness and immediacy of a description. How can you make descriptions more particular, such as pink sneakers instead of shoes? This can be especially useful when you are trying to draw your reader into the world of your story.

How can you include more info in a sentence? – *The air smelled of peppermint* vs. *a hint of peppermint mingled with the smoky air.*

CHAPTER 4: TWO STRINGS

Two Strings: *Each scene must have two separate things happening in it.*

Tying Two (or More) Strings Together
So how exactly does this Two Strings thing work?

In art, as we discussed above, we create the illusion of three dimensions with contrast. A single line forming a circle looks two-dimensional to the eye. Add shading around one side and suddenly it looks like a ball instead of a circle—as if the light were shining on the one side casting the far side into shadow. Our eye recognizes this contrast as the way real 3-D objects look and assumes that the object on the paper is 3-D, too.

What applies in art is also true in writing. Contrast, we have learned, is what makes characters three-dimensional. It is also what makes the rest of the written word spring to life: contrast in theme, contrast in plot, contrast in setting, contrast in character.

The same way that shading tricks the eye by reminding

us of what we see around us, contrast in stories reminds us of real life. In real life, things are untidy. Very seldom is anything accomplished without some difficulty. You get a new job, but you don't care for the location. You meet a nice man, but he has a girlfriend who lives far away and he has to break up with before he can really see you. You love where you live, but you miss your family who live elsewhere.

These tensions, between the realities of our life and the way we would like things to be, are what keep us striving, what make our life dramatic and interesting—interesting to others, I should say.

This is a very important point, and we should get it out of the way first thing. Stories require drama. Drama is about what is interesting to others, what is interesting to read, what is interesting to hear about.

It is *not* about what is best to live.

How Best to Live vs. How Best to Write

Having a good life—getting a job in a place you love, meeting a great fellow who is free to date, having your family move near where you live—is wonderful for those who are living it; however, it doesn't make for an interesting drama—unless it comes at the end, after a struggle to achieve it.

This is why so many romance novel publishers have a rule that the book ends with the wedding. Happy lives are less interesting to read about, even if they are better for those living them.

So, this is the first lesson of writing: *Books are never about the way we actually want things to be.*

They are never about happy people being happy. They are never about things that are just going well. They are never about creative people producing their art without obstacles.

They are never about Heaven.

You can visit Heaven in a story, as part of the contrast between what we desire and what we are stuck with day-to-day, but you could not set your whole story there, unless your story was about people in Heaven trying to help people down here on earth—where we have problems.

Drama comes from conflicts, from overcoming obstacles.

What Makes an Obstacle?

Obstacles come when there is a contrast between desired outcomes. The desired outcomes can be two desires internal to the character, such as: I want to go away to college but I also want to be near my family. Or they can be an internal vs. an external, such as: I want to bring food to my mother vs. the road has been washed out, how can I safely cross to Mother's house?

Stories come to life when this contrast becomes apparent.

Back to Two Strings

Now that we have established that stories need conflict, you may ask: "But how does all this apply to my writing? And what did you mean by 'Two Strings?'"

Have you ever heard writers talking about how they got the idea for their latest work? Often they'll say something like: *"I had this idea for the longest time about a band of clowns traveling through the desert. But it wasn't until I came up with this second idea, of a type of sand worm that only eats clowns, that the story really came alive."*

Okay, that is a horrible example. Let's try again: *I wanted to write about the life of a repair man—always hot in the summer and cold in the winter, because no one calls if the heating and air are working—but it didn't come alive until I thought: space station.*

Two different ideas are necessary to bring the story to life.

Here is an example another author recently shared with me: for a long time he wondered about what if one of the tribes who left the Tower of Babel went into space? Then, one day, his little daughter was playing princess, and he thought: what if she really was a princess? What kind of culture would hide its royalty away among normal people?

These two ideas were the two seeds—the Two Strings—needed for his novel.

A writer can have a really great idea, but until it becomes the intersection of two great ideas, it remains static, lacking in interest. As long as it is static, it is hard to write about and not very interesting to read, either.

This is why stories that read like travelogues tend to be dull. The author has one good idea: put onstage interesting places and people; however, there is no second idea to tie them together and give motion to the plot (if there even is a plot).

Sometimes, a book has at least two overarching ideas but does not necessarily have two strings to every scene. So the book is interesting, but some individual scenes still drag.

Which brings us back to the question: what do we mean by "string." By "string," in this case, I mean a concept that adds interest to the scene. Some call it a "thread." Or, put more simply: every scene should have two things going on.

Once again, it's that simple.

When we make up stories to write, we often start with

an idea: *I want to tell the story of a Hobbit name Frodo; I want to tell the story of Thomas Jefferson; I want to tell the story of a prince who marries a princess.*

Write about them doing... what?

One idea, by itself, is never enough. A single idea is like the circle made out of a single line. It may be well-drawn, but it is still flat. Without shading, it will never come to life. What is needed is a second idea to provide the contrast that brings the story alive: What if a homely Hobbit were drawn into a war story? What if Jefferson's story were told as journal entries? What if the prince has been turned into a frog?

Note that the story of Jefferson does not necessarily need a second plot idea. Jefferson's life already has events and conflicts. What it needs is an approach, something that helps the author frame the story, to choose which events to mention and how to bring his biography to life.

For example, there is an easy reader for young children called *Thomas Jefferson's Feast*. In it, the author chooses to tell us about Jefferson's life through his interaction with food: food Jefferson ate; food he encouraged others to eat, like tomatoes; food he brought to America from France. This approach is quite interesting because the overlap between the known figure, Thomas Jefferson, and this unusual subject, food during Jefferson's time, contrasts to make this short reader fascinating.

The moment the second idea, or story string, is discovered, the story springs to life. It is as if you "pull on the two strings," and the characters begin to move in the author's imagination. They stop being static and taken on a life of their own.

When characters come alive for the author, they are far more likely to come alive for the reader. This is true for a novel. This is true for a short story. This is true for every individual scene.

Ever read a book that has long passages that just don't seem to go anywhere? The characters you like are on stage. They are talking about some interesting subject, and yet... the scene seems flat, static? You have just stumbled upon a scene with only one string. The overall novel may have two or more ideas dynamically contrasting to produce a great story, but that particular scene is only accomplishing one thing.

And because it is only accomplishing one thing, there is nothing to anticipate. What do I mean by this? To go back to our baker from "Breathing Life into Characters," imagine you are reading a scene in which our favorite baker talks with his fellow bakers. You might like this baker guy a lot. You may care about whether he will recover his family after they were scattered to the four winds by the terrible baking accident, but if, in this particular scene, all the bakers talk about is baking in the same 'baker-like" way—no little child almost falling into the oven, no sudden guitar song to liven the mood, just baking—the scene becomes predictable. Your mind has nothing to surprise it and nothing to hope for, just baking.

To make that baking interesting, it has to be juxtaposed by something else: action, drama, comedy, the personal problems of bakers—something other than the one subject. Now, you may be thinking, "But I have read scenes where only one subject was discussed that were fascinating!" Go back and take a look at such a scene again and ask yourself: What else was happening in the scene?

Were the characters also doing something—making bread, preparing dinner?—something that included details that the helped give definition to the scene, perhaps even details you had not known, such as how the baker prepared a certain dish before firing it? Or that he used figs to sweeten his muffins instead of sugar? Or, perhaps it was the zany personality of the other bakers that provided the second string. While they spoke the same simple lines, there were also descriptions of how Baker Peter insisted on wearing dough on his head instead of his tall white hat, while Baker Philip sang all his lines in an operatic fashion complete with hand gestures and long-drawn-out vowels? If so, the actions or the personalities of the characters were what provided the second string that brought the scene to life.

What Do You Mean by Two Strings, Again?

Two Strings means, as in our baker example, that at least two things get accomplished. A story is a collection of different qualities, such as: plot, backstory, description, and character development. A string is one of these qualities.

Plot moves the action of the story forward. Backstory is the events that happened before the story opened that (when done well) have an impact on the events and characters. Description, if done well, makes the story more vivid and alive in the imagination of the reader. Character development helps the reader know who the character is, which, in turn, leads to a greater appreciation of the character's struggle... i.e., the story.

But put any one of these things in a scene by itself, and the scene begins to feel thin—or worse—static.

The key, then, is to mix them, to have two different contrasting purposes to the scene. Have two of these in every scene. Either touch on the threads of two different plotlines, or have the plot motion contrasted with a bit of character development, or spruce up a description by making it more particular, more interesting—possibly by having a hint of plot or character development come from how the room is described, etc.

Two Strings

All stories consist of "motion towards a goal, motion away, and motion towards it again." For example, the famous: *Boy meets girl; boy loses girl; boy gets girl.*

All good stories also consist of two strings—or threads of ideas—interacting with each other. It is often the second thread that provides the motion away and this lets the motion towards become dynamic—a story, not just a series of events. Without a second string,—or at least "motion away, motion toward"—a series of events is just a vignette.

Example:
We got in the car.
We drove up the hill.
We reached the summit.
This is not a story.

How do you turn this into the world's shortest story? Add internal dialogue. Make your internal dialogue the second thread. Make it add the motion away to make room for the back-toward.

Example:
We got in the car. *I REALLY did not want to go.*

We drove up the hill. *This must be the longest drive known to man.*

We reached the summit. *Oh my gosh! This is the most beautiful thing I've ever seen! I am so glad I agreed to come. The longest ride known to man was worth it!*

Or:

We got in the car. *My heart was heavy with sorrow.*

We drove up the hill. *I tried not to cry since I didn't want to distract my brother who was driving.*

We reached the summit. *Together we released Mom's ashes into the wind, scattering them over her favorite place in the world.*

Ladies and Gentlemen, that is the power of two strings.

Exercise: Write your own micro story
We got in the car.
We drove up the hill.
We reached the summit.

Take the above lines. For each sentence, add **one to two sentences** of thoughts or reactions that act as a counterpoint, so that this short vignette becomes a micro story.

Note: your response should be almost entirely mental. It is okay to throw in a few new actions if necessary. But the point of this exercise is that the counter-string to the physical action of the scene is the mental observations of the character. The character's thoughts, emotions, goals, and purposes should make up almost the entirety of what you are adding.

How do you do this? Ask yourself a few questions:
What is your character thinking?
Why is your character going up the hill?
What will he find there?
Does he want to go?
How can what he finds at the top be different from what he expected at the bottom?

In other words, make sure that you apply The Trick. The emotions at the end should be contrasted with those at the beginning in some way. If you write something where the emotions stay the same or where they build but do not change, it will feel like an opening instead of a complete piece.

CHAPTER 5: TO ANTICIPATE OR NOT TO ANTICIPATE?

Anticipation: *The secret to engaging readers: If the character cares, the reader cares.*

To Anticipate or Not to Anticipate?

In the first chapter, we discussed how, in the early days of Disney animation, the illustrators developed twelve principles that they discerned were necessary to produce quality animation, including *Anticipation*.

Disney and his cartoonists discovered that if a character threw a ball or put his hand in his pocket to pull out a sandwich, it often happened too quickly for the audiences' eyes to see. The viewer then did not understand where the ball had gone or where the sandwich had come from.

So the illustrators learned that they had to allow the viewer to anticipate the action. If a character was going to throw a ball, he could first be shown drawing his arm back. If he was going to pull a sandwich from his pocket, he could be shown slowly reaching out and down toward his pocket.

This way, the viewer could anticipate what was to come.

When the ball finally launched or the sandwich appeared, the viewer understood what was happening. Watching the ball sail forth into the air after a big wind up was *satisfying*.

It also meant that the animators could now surprise the viewers, often for comedic purposes. If the man with the ball drew his arm waaaaay back, wound up, and then dropped the ball behind him rather than carrying through with the throw, it was funny and, more importantly, *surprising* (at least at first).

Both *satisfaction* and *surprise* require anticipation.

If readers do not know enough to anticipate—in particular, to anticipate what kind of outcome the character *wants* —they may find the events of the story neither satisfying nor surprising.

Anticipation is Everything

When I edit, one of my jobs is to figure out why a scene does not work. I read a scene. It loses my interest. A normal person puts the book down. Not me. I have to read it regardless. My job is to tell the author how to fix it. So I sit and think very carefully about the scene. Why is it lagging? What is missing?

Nine out of ten times, what is missing is: *anticipation*

What do I mean by this? I means that the reader has nothing to look forward to. No goal has been presented that the reader cares about, so there is no particular reason to keep turning pages.

So what makes the reader care?

Diamonds Are Forever, Chickens and Pianos, too

If the reader does not know what a character wants, the

reader can't want it either. The reader has to be aware of what the character desires to achieve to be able to anticipate the character's success or failure. Otherwise, the reader is incapable of caring about whether the character gets it.

Even if the reader really, really wants to care.

To get the readers to stick around to find out what happens, you have to get them to want to know what will happen. For that to happen, the readers must have some image in their imagination of what to hope for.

Imagine the following scenario: *A damaged pirate ship captures a freighter. The freighter contains as cargo: a piano, a chicken, and a thousand diamonds.*

Scenario 1)

The pirates arrive. They look around. They see the diamonds. They chuckle and hi-five each other. They go on to their next event.

Was that satisfying?

Hmm.

Not really.

Let's try:

Scenario 2)

The pirates arrive.

"Look sharp," said Jake. "Look for anything we can salvage. A chair. An old wine bottle. With our base gone and our ship damaged, if we can't find enough for a little repair work..." He trails off.

"What's it matter, Captain?" said Tuck, rubbing his stubble. "Even if we scrape together enough for a few repairs, we've lost the diamond mine. Without weapons-grade diamonds, we have no weapons. Without weapons, we'll never break through the barricade." The old pirate pulls his pocket watch from his tattered coat and rubs the initials on the tarnished silver cover. "Sorry, Ma."

Swishing beside him, as beautiful as she was deadly, Kashvi threw the trail of her pink and yellow sari over one shoulder. In her thick accent, she murmured sweetly, "I am so sorry, Tuck. We worked so hard, for so many months, to gain the antidote... and now we will never be able to deliver it in time."

Tuck glared at Ricky, who was dawdling in the rear. "If the kid hadn't burned out our final crystals on his infernal invention..."

Ricky hung his head sheepishly, "How was I to know we'd lose the mine? The worst thing is... it actually works. I fixed it. We could be using it. Selling it... making millions. But now... without more diamonds? When will we ever even have a chance to demonstrate it to somebody?"

"Lotta good it'll do us now," growled Tuck. His face fell, glum. "Lotta good it will do my old mum."

The group moved forward dejectedly, shoulders slumped. They rounded the corner, Shari in the lead.

"Boys..." Kashvi's jaw dropped. She jumped up and down rubbing her palms together, her face shining with in joy. "Look! Look!"

Around the corner, next to an old piano and a chicken—shimmering like a dream—rose an enormous pile of shining, glittering, weapons-grade diamonds.

Scenario 3)

The pirates stumbled off the ship. They were scarecrow

thin and haggard. They rushed around the freighter, searching, peering. One found a water spout and drank thirstily.

"Guys, diamonds!" called one pirate.

The rest of the crew stumbled into the room, too weary to care.

"Big deal," said a haggard old spacer, sitting down on the piano bench. "We won't live to make it back to market to sell it. We…"

He stopped. There was a noise. A scuffling of talons. From around the heaping mound of the diamonds shuffled a chicken.

"Food!" cried the pirate, leaping to his feet.

The pirates fell upon the chicken and dragged it back to their ship's kitchen, feathers flying. Even before they reached their ship, one had already twisted off the bird's foot and began gnawing on it.

With food, they would live long enough to make it back to civilization, where they could sell the diamonds and repair their ship.

They were saved.

Scenario 4)

Kirth Gerson* stepped onto the freighter, examining his environment. The crew was dead. There was little to salvage. The cargo hold was filled with diamonds. His experienced eye glanced over them calculating their value—about as much as his magazine brought in during a single month of circulation.

He circled the diamonds. A chicken ran by him. He raised an eyebrow and then ignored the scrawny bird.

Then he saw it. Sitting in the corner.

His grandmother's piano.

Slowly, Gerson walked across the room and ran his hand across its dusty but polished surface. It was exactly as he remembered it. He ran a finger along the scratch he had put there the day he crashed into it when pretending he was fighting a splegasaurus. How Grandpa had walloped him. He remembered Grandma playing at the keyboard, her face suffused with joy.

She had been playing when the Five Demon Princes descended upon Mt. Pleasant and slaughtered everyone... including her.

Gerson touched the instrument once more. Then he turned and walked toward the bridge. Somewhere, there would be a record as to where the crew of the freighter had picked up the piano. He need only follow it backward and yet another clue as to the whereabouts of the remaining Demon Princes would be his.

As he strode purposefully, a ghost of a smile quirked at his grim lips. He was one step closer to his final revenge.

When you write a scene, you want to clue your readers in as to what your characters need—so that by the time they reach the cargo bay, the reader knows whether to cheer for the diamonds, for the piano, or for the chicken.

Anticipation: it's as easy as that.

From this we learn the first all-important tenet of the world of the story:

> *If the character cares, the reader cares.*

Once the reader cares, there is something about the story to anticipate, and that is what we mean by *being interested*.

* Kirth Gerson – the hero of Jack Vance's *Demon Princes* series. His home town of Mt. Pleasant was destroyed by five super criminals. He and his grandfather are the only survivors. His grandfather raises him with the sole purpose of hunting down the culprits and taking revenge. (If you have not read the series, run out and get it! It is excellent, though it does not include a scene with a piano, a chicken, and diamonds.)

What Is Plot without Anticipation?

Author Sarah A. Hoyt learned this lesson the hard way. In her excellent essay, "The Shadows of What's to Come", she writes:

When I was a young writer, verdant as spring lettuce, writing my novels on the hope of publication, and sending them forth to publishers who'd never heard of me, my most common rejection was that "your novel just meanders and has no plot."

This puzzled the living heck out of me. In those days I was a plotter, because I was insecure. Not only did I outline and diagram ahead of time, but I ruthlessly (too ruthlessly) trimmed everything that didn't advance the plot or reinforce the theme or whatever.

...

Being told I had no plot was one of those things. It would be like you leaving home in the morning, and everyone telling you that you were purple. After a while, you decide you can't see your own color, and I decided I knew nothing about plotting and started stealing structure/plot from other books. (No, this is not plagiarism. It is at worst stupid.)

After many years of suffering so, she finally saw a glimpse of the sky through the clouds:

It took me years—and six novels out—before I was whining to Dave Freer about how I couldn't plot for beans, and couldn't seem to learn it, since I couldn't SEE what I was missing, when he said "Your plots and structure are fine, but you have to learn to foreshadow, woman.

He then recommended I read Georgette Heyer to learn techniques and that worked somewhat, but mostly what worked was my being aware of the need to give the reader advance warning WITHOUT spoiling the surprise.

That was part of the problem, see. I thought every new plot development had to be a SURPRISE —I don't know where I got the idea, frankly—and the more surprise the better. So I must not give away what was coming. Not even by hints.

I recommend the entire essay. You can find it online at Mad Genius Club: https://madgeniusclub.com/2017/07/05/the-shadows-of-whats-to-come/

In Conclusion

If the first all-important tenet of storytelling is: *If the character cares, the reader cares.* The second-most important tenet follows: The reader must be able to *anticipate* what is to come—rightly or wrongly—before they are capable of caring about the outcome.

Exercise A:

Pick an event in your story where your character overcomes an obstacle, a fight scene, an action scene, a romantic encounter. Establish near the beginning of the scene what it is that the character hopes to achieve by overcoming this obstacle.

Follow through by making additional references back to this, if needed, throughout the scene. Have the character's emotional response to the outcome of the attempt—success or failure—correspond to whether or not those hopes are achieved.

Exercise B:

Try writing the same scene as if the character has a different motivation for this particular obstacle. (Example: version one, he wants to save the girl. Version two, he's angry and wants to clean his opponent's clock. Or he's hungry and really wants to get to the next peaceful spot and have something to eat, images of juicy steaks and warm bread with melting butter and honey dancing in his head. Or he's tricky and is only approaching the obstacle to trick his opponent into believing some false thing. Maybe he wants to lose, so that he can give his opponent a gift without offending the other's pride? Etc.)

Pick from among possible motives for the character or brainstorm for new ones.

Which version of scene do you like best?

CHAPTER 6: THE ULTIMATE SECRET

The Ultimate Secret: *The secret to making every story—and scene—engaging and satisfying is to give the reader a glimpse of the character's purpose.*

The Power of Chocolate

Some years ago, when I first started editing, I ran into an interesting phenomenon. Occasionally, I would sit down to edit a manuscript, and it would be excruciatingly boring. I could hardly get myself to read to the next page. There was no way in the universe or outside of it that I would have kept reading that book if I had not been being paid to so do.

Sometimes, it got so bad that I had to bribe myself with chocolate to continue.

Then I would reach the end of the book, and a funny thing would happen. I would sit back and think about what I just read and think, *"Boy, that's a good book!"*

What had just happened?

Dutifully, I would sit down and work out in my head what made the story good, when I looked at it as a whole.

Then I would write notes for the author, advising them as to how they could get the interesting stuff onstage early on. Somewhere around the third or fifth time this happened, I discovered something interesting… I was giving each author the same advice.

Oh, not the same specific advice. Obviously, the specifics were tailored for the individual story. But the general overall advice was the same. In fact, in the years since then, maybe one or two manuscripts have passed my desk that I did not feel needed this particular piece of advice.

It seemed to be the number one error made by beginning, and some not-so-beginning, authors.

What was this advice? I will share it with you, but first we need to review two principles.

Why We Read

When we pick up a book, why do we continue reading? Why do we make the effort to turn the pages? Why do we keep reading rather than playing video games, chatting on social media, watching movies, shopping, polishing our toenails, or the many, many other things we could do in life?

There are many possible responses, but they can all be reduced to something we discussed in the previous chapter: *We want to know what is going to happen next.*

What is it, then, that makes what happens next matter?

Caring Is… Caring

Imagine two stories, both of which include a scene involving the local swim team:

In Story A, the main character drops off her child for a swim team meet on her way to an important meeting, where she and others will decide whether or not to take up arms against the tyrant who rules their town.

In Story B, the main character's son is on the swim team. He loves swim team. He adores swim team. He lives for swim team. His feelings are hurt one day when his team swims against the Sharks, a neighboring team, and he loses to a rude boy from the next town who mocks him.

On the way home, the family is in a car accident. The boy is badly injured. Doctors tell him that he will never walk again. The boy is dejected. He won't talk or even eat on his own.

His mother has an idea. She begs to be allowed to take him to the pool. His doctors are doubtful that this is wise. Yet, despite the objections of all around her, his mother prevails. She carries her teenage boy into the local gym and gently puts him into the pool.

Once in the pool, the boy comes to life. Swimming a little every day, he regains his strength.

In three months, he is walking again. In six, he is back on the swim team.

The day comes when his team will again face the Sharks. The boy has recovered to such a degree that his mother believes he might actually be able to beat his old rival. She watches from the bleachers, her fingers crossed, as the race begins.

Now the $64,000 Question is: In which story are you, the reader, more interested in the outcome of the swim meet? Why?

One might reply: *"B, because in that story the swim meet is more important?"*

To which I must ask, *"Important to whom?"*

To you? You who have bills to pay, school work to do, a job you need to perform, health concerns, life concerns?

Does the outcome of an imaginary swim meet truly matter to you? Will it improve your life?

No.

It matters, because it is important to *the character*.

Here again, we are reminded of the two all-important tenets of storytelling that we discussed in the previous chapter:

Anticipation

and

If the character cares, the reader cares.

The Ultimate Secret

Readers read books when they care about what will happen.

Yep, folks, it really is that simple.

The first thing that makes the reader care what happens is if the character cares. If the character really cares about something, anything, the reader tends to start caring, too. The easiest way to show that a character cares is: *Have the character have a goal.*

Have the characters have goals they *really* care about and —and here is the most important part—put that goal *as close* to *the beginning of the book as possible.*

If possible, put it on the opening page, or at least in the opening scene.

Why?

Oh, Now I See What You Did There!

Taking a step back, let us answer an early question, namely how could a book be dull while one was reading it and yet good at the end? The answer to this was simple: *Most writers discover their story as they go.*

The late Sir Terry Pratchett described writing as seeing a series of peaks surrounded by mist and then wandering between the peaks to discover what was in the foggy valleys. His peaks were the major plot points of the story and his misty-filled valleys were the discoveries that authors make as they go.

Many of these discoveries include: who the main character truly is; what the main character's real motivation is; why the character cares about this goal; etc.

Once the reader learns these things, the story becomes quite dramatic! Problem is, many authors only make these things up as they approach the end of their manuscript. Reading their first draft felt like slogging through a muddy bog.

Imagine if I had told you about the swim meet first, droning on about who did what in which lane of the pool, with no introductions, and only at the end of the book did you learn that the boy had been mocked, been in an accident, told he would never walk again, lost hope, recovered his will to live, and made it back to swim again!

In retrospect, you would probably find that touching—problem is, chances are you would never had read that far, because nothing before that point made the swim meet matter.

This is why the goal needs to go as close to the beginning of the story as humanly possible. When the character cares about a goal, the reader starts to care, too. The more the character cares, the more the readers care. The more the readers care, the more they turn pages, eager to discover whether or not the character achieves that goal.

Put your reason to care right up front, where the readers can find it right away!

Choosing the Goal

How do we choose what goal to have our character living and longing for? This goal should be related to whatever the character achieves at the end of the book. It does not, however, have to be directly related. For one thing, the character's goal may need to grow or change as the story continues.

Characters might start out with a simple or selfish goal, and it could expand as the character's horizons expand. Or they might change their goal because of increased wisdom, putting aside an outgrown purpose for one that is more realistic or more noble. Either way, though, there should be a direct chain of cause and effect between the original goal and the final one.

A goal can be something straightforward, such as *I want to save my brother* in a book where the plot concerns the brother's kidnapping. More often, however, the goal provides the second string—setting up the second, conflicting tension for the story. Imagine, in the story just mentioned about the kidnapped brother, if the character's goal was that she was tired of being lonely and *wanted a family*.

When her brother goes missing, she throws herself heart and soul into rescuing him, but she still feels alone. Then, by the end, not only has she recovered her brother, but she has also fallen in love with the man who aids her in finding him, and he proposes, fulfilling her desire for a family of her own—the story's secondary goal, but the character's primary desire.

To choose a goal, look at what occurs at the end of the story and pick something that leads to it, directly or indirectly, that your character can care about at the beginning.

Why Is a Goal the Ultimate Secret?
Remember our two tenets of the world of the story: *Caring is Caring* and *Anticipation*? Adding a goal forwards both of these!

First, a goal gives the reader something to care about.

Second, a goal helps the reader anticipate.

Giving the character a goal and then checking in with it every so often—so the reader can see how the character is getting on with the goal—acts as a mile marker. It helps the reader to gauge how the plot is progressing and to anticipate the next step. If the character stops at least two or three times during the story to think about his goal and how close or far he is from it, it helps the reader stay on target. The reader can now see how the actions going on around the character lead toward or away from the goal the character is trying to reach.

It is like being on a road trip and looking out the window to see that you just passed mile marker thirty-three on a seventy-six-mile trip. You suddenly know how far you have come and how far you still have to go.

You can anticipate when you will arrive.

Maybe you will be correct, or maybe something unexpected will occur to alter your path. But, if you don't anticipate any ETA, you cannot be satisfied when you make it or surprised when you do not.

An additional benefit is that, depending on your goal, it can also give you a ready-made second string, especially if your character's goal is related to a secondary issue that is not the main quest of the story.

Proof That It Works

This add-a-goal technique is both easy and effective. Let me give you an example:

When I set out to write my fourth *Book of Unexpected Enlightenment,* I had a particular ending in mind. Sadly, it turned out that reaching that point in the plot would make the book far too long. I had to cut the book in half at a random spot.

I chose a spot that had some action I could turn into climactic battle, but I was not really satisfied with it. Then I thought *"Gee, I give authors advice about goals all the time. I wonder if I could apply that advice to this book?"*

I read the new end and chose a goal I could put in the first chapter that pointed toward this conclusion. Then, I went through the new book and picked out a few spots where I could add a line or two that brought out that plotline—a mile marker. I also added an additional short scene to support the new ending.

The result? Reviewers have claimed that *The Awful Truth About Forgetting* was my *"most focused book yet."* This even though it was actually the least focused, since it was randomly cut in half. By setting up a goal the character cared about that pointed toward my conclusion—and checking in with it occasionally—I allowed the reader the freedom to anticipate, thus leading to a more satisfying reading experience.

Adding a goal, and occasionally coming back to visit it, really works!

Exercise A: Prep Exercise 1

Examine your story. Write down a few lines about what is achieved at the end.

For instance, imagine you were writing the movie *The Court Jester*. (NOTE: if you haven't watched *The Court Jester* with Danny Kaye, drop everything and go watch it now. You won't regret it, and the film is more fun without spoilers. Also, we are going to refer to it again in a later chapter, so you might as well watch it. Go ahead. This book will still be here when you come back.)

If you were examining *The Court Jester*, you might write (Warning: **Spoilers**):

The Black Fox triumphs.

The baby is returned to the throne.

The princess falls for the grim, grisly, gruesome Griswold after all.

Hawkins lives and is united with Maid Jean.

Now, take your own work and make a similar list of what your character achieves by the end of your story.

Exercise B: Prep Exercise 2

Make a list of goals your character could have that might lead to your ending.

Examples from *The Court Jester* (no spoilers):

The Black Fox wants to restore the baby to the throne.

The princess wants true love.

Hawkins wants to do daring deeds and win the heart of Maid Jean.

Exercise C: Goals!

Pick from the list you made during the previous exercise the goal that you feel works best. Write a line or paragraph that expresses this idea. Find a place in the first few pages of your manuscript where you can insert this goal.

Requirement: The goal as it appears in your story must include a word that indicates that this is something the character *wants*. It is not good enough to merely include the idea as a character trait. The reader will not grasp that this is a desired thing. Include a word that states clearly that the goal is desired, such as: *wanted, longed for, dreamed of, vowed, sought.*

Example (words that convey to the reader that this is a goal in bold):

Carla was **tired** of living alone. She **longed** for a friend, a companion to share her dreams with. Heck, she would have settled for a cat.

Or

Sarah Hopkins sat in the bleachers **biting her nails. More than anything** she had ever **wanted** in her whole life, she wanted her son to win this race. Just this one race. *Give me this,* **God, she begged,** *and I will never ask for anything again.*

Or

Ash Ketchum might only be ten, but he **loved** Pokemon **more than** any other little boy ever had loved them. It was his **dream** to become a Pokemon Master. He was going to catch them all!

Bonus Exercise D: Roadmarkers

Pick three places in your Work In Progress (often referred to as WIP) where your character can pause and think about the goal and write a paragraph or two where he or she does so. The reflection can be positive *"Look how close I have come to the mark!"* or negative *"At this rate, I'll never get there."*

Examples (Spoilers for The Court Jester):

Positive: The Black Fox declares, *"Yes, Maid Jean writes that she has the key. It is only a matter of hours now!"*

Negative: The Black Fox pauses and shakes his head. *"The secret tunnel has caved in. Only a child could fit through that tiny hole. Alas, Hawkins is lost."*

Or:

Hawkins could rejoice in one scene that Maid Jean loves him, despair in the next that she is now the captive of the king, and, in yet a third, bemoan that he must die before he can marry her.

Write some roadmarks like this for your characters and their goals. Try to space these literary milestones somewhat evenly throughout your story.

PART TWO: THE CRAFT OF WRITING
REFINING THE CRAFT

CHAPTER 7: ENGAGING OPENINGS

Open with a Hook: *The best way to hook the reader is to leave him with a question that is not answered until deep into the work.*

What Is an Opening?
Or rather, what is its purpose?
Short answer: *to intrigue the reader.*
That is the number-one purpose of an opening. To draw readers in and make them curious about what is going to come next. If they are not curious, they will not continue reading.
Many of you know the most famous of opening lines: *It was a dark and stormy night*, but have you read the entire sentence?
"It was a dark and stormy night; the rain fell in torrents—except at occasional intervals, when it was checked by a violent gust of wind which swept up the streets (for it is in London that our scene lies), rattling along the housetops, and fiercely agitating the scanty flame of the lamps that struggled against the darkness."

From *Paul Clifford* by Edward Bulwer-Lytton

Paul Clifford is a pulpy novel about a man who is a gentleman by day and a master criminal by night, but that is probably not why you have heard of its opening line, which may be the most-mocked first line in the universe. The first phrase of it was often quoted by Snoopy from *Peanuts* in his literary efforts. It has also sparked a writing contest known as the Bulwer-Lytton Fiction Contest where people compete to write the worst opening line of the year. (Some of them are very amusing. You can find out more here: *https://www.bulwer-lytton.com/*)

Incidentally, *"It was a dark and stormy night"* is also the opening to the classic science fiction children's novel, *A Wrinkle in Time*.

Let's examine a few more opening lines:

Call me Ishmael.—Herman Melville, *Moby-Dick*

It is a truth universally acknowledged, that a single man in possession of a good fortune, must be in want of a wife.—Jane Austen, *Pride and Prejudice*

Happy families are all alike; every unhappy family is unhappy in its own way.—Leo Tolstoy, *Anna Karenina* (translated by Constance Garnett)

It was the best of times, it was the worst of times, it was the age of wisdom, it was the age of foolishness, it was the epoch of belief, it was the epoch of incredulity, it was the season of Light, it was the season of Darkness, it was the spring of hope, it was the winter of despair.—Charles Dickens, *A Tale of Two Cities*

Scarlett O'Hara was not beautiful, but men seldom realized it when caught by her charm as the Tarleton twins were. —Margaret Mitchell, *Gone With The Wind*

The human race, to which so many of my readers belong, has been playing at children's games from the beginning, and will probably do it till the end, which is a nuisance for the few people who grow up.—G. K. Chesterton, *The Napoleon of Notting Hill*

Taran wanted to make a sword; but Coll, charged with the practical side of his education, decided on horseshoes.—Lloyd Alexander, *The Book of Three*

This is my favorite book in the world, though I have never read it. —William Goldman, *The Princess Bride*

After an eternity, it was beginning to end.—Roger Zelazny, *Nine Princes in Amber*

A snazzy first line that catches people's attention is a great start. Openings, however, are about more than just first lines. Intriguing the reader is the first purpose of an opening, but it has other purposes as well. Specifically: *to set the scene and introduce the story.*

First, we want our readers to give our book a chance. Then, we want them to *keep* reading.

To accomplish this, we must draw the reader into the story. We need to set up, right at the beginning, enough of the story that the readers will be able to figure out whether or not this is the kind of story in which they are interested. This is, in part, a matter of hooking the readers, but it is also a matter of convincing them that the setting and characters will continue to be of interest to them over the duration of an entire work.

After all, they could be playing a video game, watching a movie, taking a long walk, or buffing their navel. People have *a lot* of claims upon their attention today, and many books from which to choose.

If we want them to read ours, we have to both hook them and keep them on the line. The greatest opening in the universe won't reel in readers who have decided they are not interested in that type of story. This means we have very few words to make readers curious enough that they want to stay around.

So how do we do this with the fewest number of words?

The Opening Workshop:

Sci-fi author Allen L. Wold runs a workshop on writing openings at science fiction conventions. He has worked it out to a simple exercise, which he has given me permission to share with you. This is the exercise we are going to work on today.

Allen Wold's exercise is: Write a hundred words of the opening of a story. Within these hundred words, you must include a *hook*, a *character*, and a *setting*.

. . .

Hook:

Now you may be asking—because I know I did for years—what is a hook? What does Mr. Wold, or any writing instructor, mean by this term?

Let's look at a couple more openings:

It was a bright cold day in April, and the clocks were striking thirteen.—George Orwell, *1984*

Why is the clock striking 13? Is it military time? Is Doctor Who arriving? How did the clocks come to have thirteen on them? Is it a fantasy or just something alien to our experience?

Those questions? They are the "hook"—the thing that makes us want to know more about what is going on.

There was a boy called Eustace Clarence Scrubb, and he almost deserved it.—C. S. Lewis, *The Voyage of the Dawn Treader*

I don't know about you, but I find myself very curious about why he almost deserves it!

So, what is a hook? A hook, in writing terms, is an *unanswered* question. The point of an opening is to hook readers—so that they keep reading. Such hooks come in three kinds.

Opening Line Hook—a terrific opening line that amuses or wows the reader. This will not carry the book, but if readers are intrigued or amused enough, they may keep reading for a while, based merely on the power of the opening line. This grants the author more time to truly hook them.

Compelling Prose Hook—some good books don't have WOW opening lines, but the prose is compelling. Usually, the things being described are specific and unexpected. This may be because of the subject matter or the elegance of the word choice. Either way, an intriguing opening can convince a reader to keep turning the page.

Propelling Hook—the third kind of hook, and in some ways the most desirable kind, is an opening that propels the reader forward into the story itself. It asks a strong question that can only be answered by reading more. Not every opening is going to have the kind of hook that propels the reader into the first chapter and beyond, but if you can achieve that, you really draw in your readers!

Occasionally, a truly brilliant or divinely-inspired author combines the first and third hook—producing a first line that is both intriguing and compelling. That is an ideal way to open a book, but if you cannot think of the perfect line, don't despair. Many, many good books lack a zinger of a first line and yet still manage to hook the reader within the first few paragraphs.

I had the honor of helping with Mr. Wold's Openings Workshop several of times. Many times, a participant would write a very charming paragraph, with an engaging character and an intriguing setting, but Mr. Wold would still declared the paragraph to have failed to meet the qualifications. Why?

Because it was finished. The question posed in the opening was answered by the end of the hundred words. There was no hook.

Let's take a look at the other two requirements of Mr. Wold's exercise:

Setting:

As we covered in the earlier chapter on Description, your readers are like people floating in sensory deprivation tanks. They know nothing about your world except for what you tell them. They can sense nothing except what you describe. You want to help ground them in the world of your story as soon as possible, to provide stimulus that will help them orient as to where they are—both the time and place.

In particular, you want to let them know:

Does this story take place in the modern world? (If so, what country or state or town—as applicable?)

Does it take place in the past or future?

Does it take place on a different world, and, if so, what is the name of that world? What kind of a world is it—science fiction or fantasy?

A good beginning delivers whatever the reader needs to be oriented as to the time and place of the story.

Even *It was a dark and stormy night* has a setting— London... *a violent gust of wind which swept up the streets (for it is in* **London** *that our scene lies)...*

Character:

Why character? Why specifically must a character be

named in the opening exercise? Because character is what truly engages us in a story. *If the character cares, we care.*

Simple as that.

The character is our eyes and our ears. They signal to us what we should think and love, what we should dread and fear. We don't know what to hope for, what to anticipate, unless there is someone to hint this to us, preferably someone who wants something.

Because, again, if the character cares, we care. Or, more specifically, if the character doesn't care, you can be sure that the reader won't either!

Now, some of you may be thinking of specific stories you have read where it was not the character that drew you in. It was, say, the setting. In such cases, the setting itself is usually almost a character. It is portrayed with such care and personality that it serves the role of character in that opening. This, however, is difficult to achieve and dangerous, as if you don't do it extraordinarily well, you run the risk of not engaging your readers.

Example of an Opening:

This is an actual opening line written during one of Allen Wold's workshops. (Mr. Wold insists upon the rule that everyone in the room who is not part of the judge's panel must participate, including any professional authors who happen to be present.):

It was not the being dead that I minded, it was the hours.—John C. Wright, "Pale Realms of Shade"

. . .

I don't recall exactly how much of the opening of "Pale Realms of Shade" was written at the workshop. Some of this may have been added later, but here are the first few paragraphs. Notice that more questions are raised than answered:

It was not the being dead that I minded, it was the hours.

No one ever calls me up during the day, and most people decide to wait until after midnight, for some reason. I am a morning person, or was, so meetings in the still, dark hours lost between midnight and the dawn made me crabby.

This time, it was not some comfortable séance room or picturesque graveyard with moss-covered stone angels. I came to the surface of mortal time on a street corner of some American city, mid-Twentieth to early Twenty-First Century. You can tell from the height of the buildings that it is American, and from the fact that the road names are written on signs rather than walls. And Twenty-Second Century streets are not lit up at night, of course.

The main road was called Saint Street. The small alley was called Peter Way. Great. I was crossed by Saint and Peter.

I smelled her perfume before I saw her. I turned. There she was, outlined against the streetlamp beyond. I could not mistake her silhouette: slender, alluring, like a she-panther as she walked.

"Matthias," she breathed in her low whisper. Her voice was throbbing music to me, despite everything that had happened. "You look well—ah—considering."

"Lorelei," I grunted. She was just wearing a blouse and skirt and a knee-length gray coat, but on her the outfit could have made the cover of a fashion magazine. Or a girly magazine. Her wild mass of gold-red hair was like a waterfall of bright fire tumbling past her shoulders to the small of her back. Atop, like a cherry on strawberry ice-cream, was perched a brimless cap. My

arms ached with the desire to take her and hold her. But I could never touch her, or, for that matter, anyone ever again.

She sighed and rolled her enormous emerald-green eyes. "Sweetheart, this time, you have to tell me if you were murdered. You have to!"

I took a puff of an imaginary cigarette, and watched the smoke, equally imaginary, drift off in a plume more solid than I was. "I ain't saying."

Here we have an opening hook, a setting, an amusing noir character, and a number of unanswered questions: including: *Why is he dead? Why is he still around? Who just called him up? And why won't he tell her whether or not he was murdered?*

When you write an opening, look for ways to ask questions that are not answered immediately, or which are answered by something that leads to yet another unanswered question.

Open Active

Open active: Start the scene with changes underway and then explain how you got there… unless the changes are significant.

Here, we are discussing a technique that can be used for internal openings—the beginnings to new chapters and scenes. This technique could also be applied to first lines, but first lines have additional issues weighing upon them, additional information they need to convey, that do not apply to interior openings.

An active opening is when you start your scene in the middle of the action, where something interesting is already going on, instead of with a bridging scene that connects the previous scene to the next scene.

Active openings are also called *In Medias Res*, which, for the Latin Illiterate (such as myself) is a phrase meaning something like *"in the middle of the affair."*

Just to make sure we are all on the same page, here are two examples of openings—one active, one not:

1) *The next day, we rose early and washed the car. After that, we headed down Route 66.*

2) *"He's gaining on us! Step on it!" Carly yelled. She hung half out the passenger window, so that when I swerved around the rolling oil drum, she nearly fell out of the car.*

Which of those beginnings do you find more interesting?

Most readers would choose the second option. Why? Two reasons: First, the active opening sentence is often more interesting in and of itself. (See above.) Second, and more importantly, it raises questions—a.k.a. hooks: *What is going on? Why is this happening? Who is chasing them?* The more questions the reader asks—assuming that they have faith that the author will provide the answers—the more eager the reader is to read on.

There is another benefit as well. Starting in the middle often makes the whole scene that follows more interesting. It jumps right to the exciting part, skipping the more drab lead up. This helps keep the plot on track and moving quickly.

There are two keys to an active opening: picking an arresting starting place and filling in the gap.

. . .

Picking an Arresting Starting Place

Picking a scene that will draw the reader's interest requires that you think out the events you want to have happen and then pick a moment from them that is early enough that the main action has not happened yet, and yet far enough along that the action has already begun.

The action does not need to have fully begun. In the above example, instead of starting with the chase, I could have started with:

"There's a red Honda following us." Carly leaned out the window, her hand shading her eyes. *"Does that mean anything to you?"*

This beginning is also active—far more active than the first example above—but it requires less explanation for the reader to grasp how the main characters reached this spot, which leads us to…

Filling in the Gaps

Jumping into the middle of the scene means you have to go back at some point and explain what happened between the previous scene and the current action—how the characters came to be in this exciting predicament. Usually, this is done through a mini-flashback in the first few paragraphs of the new scene. You don't want to wait too long, as you don't want the readers sense of puzzlement to grow to the point that it interferes with their enjoyment. So, unless the way the character got into this situation is a secret you are withholding for a good reason, you want to get it out of the way as soon as possible.

The key to a good active opening is being able to do this elegantly. Going back to our example above, pretend for a moment that one of the pieces of information you need to put across is that the characters recently washed their car. If so, include it in the mini-flashback.

"He's gaining on us! Step on it!" Carly yelled. She hung half out the passenger window, so that when I swerved around the rolling oil drum, she nearly fell out of the car.

Cutting hard to the right to avoid the oncoming truck, I barreled through a puddle, splashing mud all over our newly-washed car.

Or even:

"He's gaining on us! Step on it!" Carly yelled. She hung half out the passenger window, so that when I swerved around the rolling oil drum, she nearly fell out of the car.

I cut hard to the right, avoiding an oncoming truck. We had risen early this morning so we could wash the car before setting out. At the time, it had not occurred to me that they might find us during the trip, so we had not brought our weapons. If they caught us, all we had to defend ourselves with was my little brother's soccer cleat that he left in the back seat by mistake and an old umbrella.

Here you see an example of a rapid opening followed by a bit of backstory, just enough to fill in the gaps as to what the character did since the last scene.

. . .

When Do You Use an Active Opening?

Whenever you can. Action is more interesting than static. Which leads to the next question: when do you not open actively?

There are a number of instances when an active opening is not desirable. Some reasons include: the complexity of the events jumped, the subject of the scene, and variation.

Complexity

If many events have taken place since the last scene, it may be impossible to write a quick, elegant mini-flashback. It is easy to cover getting up and washing the car, or running into town and going shopping before heading to the rendezvous, but if the villains showed up, killed the main character's parakeet, burnt down her house, and kidnapped her mother-in-law before the big fight scene, that is a little harder to sum up.

Basically, the rule of thumb is: If the explanation of how they got there is so long or awkward as to slow down the current scene, you would probably be better off writing the events in chronological order.

Scene Subject

If the subject of the scene is not active, there is no point in confusing the reader by starting in the middle. A quiet walk in the garden with the family parakeet (before the villains arrive to off the dear bird*) does not need an active beginning. While it would still be nice to open with an interesting or evocative line, it does not need to be *in medias res*.

*Do not fear, Dear Parakeet Lovers, our feathered heroine is not daunted by this dire turn of events. She comes back as a ghost to help her owner escape the underground lair!

Variation

Even if all your scenes have dramatic action (i.e., while walking in the garden with the cat, the main character activates a trip wire that opens a trap door, dropping him into the center of a fight going on in the underground headquarters of the villain) it is sometimes nice to start a scene with a in-depth description or a gentle moment merely for the sake of variation.

Readers need breathers as well as action. A moment taken sniffing the hyacinths and feeling the breeze that is ruffling the parakeet's feathers can make the surprise drop into the busy secret underground headquarters even more unexpected.

How much breather vs. action—how many scenes to open in the midst of things vs. otherwise—depends upon your genre. For instance, a romance would be likely to have more gentle scene openings than a thriller.

Conclusion

In closing, starting your scenes with a bang helps jump-start your readers into what is to come, compelling them to keep reading. Then—so long as you have a compelling middle and you are able to end on another bang—your story will be irresistible.

Do all first lines have to follow Wold's formula? No, of course not. There is no writing rule, no matter how tried and true, that you can't find someone who has broken it and yet made it work. However, there is also a reason why "tried and true" is tried and true.

If you do follow his formula, your chances of catching your readers' attention increases dramatically. Try it for yourself!

Exercise A:

Write several opening lines for the same story.

Exercise B:

Write an opening. Make sure that each one mentions a setting, a specific location, and a character, and that it includes an unanswered question. It should be no more than 100 words, 200 at most.

Exercise C:

Write an opening, as long or short as you like. It should have:

1) A good opening line

2) A hook near the beginning to encourage readers to keep reading.

3) An interesting subject in the opening scene that follows the first line

4) A hook by the end of the scene—leaving an unanswered question that makes readers want to keep reading to find the answer. (The later in the story the question gets

answered, the better, as that one question could keep them reading for hours.)

Exercise D:

Take the opening you wrote above and make it more active. Start later in the story.

Exercise E:

Start earlier back: set up more of the scene before introducing the real action. Start the previous day, or seven years earlier, or when the main character was two.

CHAPTER 8: PLOT WE'VE GOT...

Plot: *Ask yourself: How can I make this more...*

Plot

What exactly do we mean by plot? When we use the word *plot*, we often mean three distinct things:
Concept or Idea
Sequence of Events
Anticipation

Let's take a look at an example of each one.

Concept or Idea
Godzilla vs. Alice in Wonderland on the Moon.

Sequence of Events
Alice is bored at a party.

Alice walks down to the water's edge.

Alice discovers that she can walk on the silvery reflection of the moon on the water.

This leads her to the moon.

The moon is peopled by living letters of the alphabet.

Baby i is particularly eerie, since its head floats above its shoulders.

The King of the Alphabet is A, who is at war with Z.

Z has stolen some monsters from earth, in order to terrorize the rest of the alphabet.

One of these monsters turns out to be Godzilla.

Etc.

Anticipation

Alice longs for something beyond the boredom of the everyday, so when she finds herself on a fanciful adventure, the reader doesn't know what is coming, but they are pleased that Alice has this opportunity to accomplish her wish. Alice loves animals, but when she goes to see Z's new animals, things take an unexpected turn.

And that is the key: *Things take an unexpected turn*—the turn cannot be *unexpected* unless the reader is *expecting* something else.

Sequence of Events

Donald Maass's *Writing the Breakout Novel* has some really good advice and exercises on this topic. One of my favorites is called: *What could make it worse?*

What could make it worse?

Let's say you have an event: Your character is about to take a test. Ask yourself: *What could make it worse?*

> If he doesn't pass, he loses the chance at an internship with his childhood hero, a chance that will never come again.

Then, ask yourself: *what could make that worse?*

> Maybe he runs into someone and coffee gets spilled all over his last-minute study notes?

Then, ask yourself: *what could make that worse?*

> As he is going into the test, he receives a call that a dear family member has just been in an accident. Now he is worried.

Then, ask yourself: *what could make that worse?*

> A sudden freak storm downs a tree that cuts out the electricity. Now he has to take the test in the dark.

Maass recommends asking at least seven to ten times. However, Maass's take is a bit limited. A thriller might need to get worse and worse, but what if you are writing a different kind of story?

What Could Make It More...

Maass's exercise is limited to "What could make it worse?" This can be useful, but for some stories, it becomes a bit limited. Personally, I prefer *"What could make it more interesting?"*

While things getting worse often makes the story more interesting, occasionally something getting suddenly better can also make a story more interesting. When planning our plots, unexpectedly good occurrences can be as enthralling as bad ones.

But what if you are writing a tearjerker? Then ask yourself: *What could make it sadder?* And then ask yourself this again and again and again.

What if it is a romance? Then you might ask yourself: *What could make it more romantic?* A comedy? *What could make it funnier?* Funnier than that? Funnier again? Nearing the end of your work? Maybe you would benefit from: *What could make this happier?* And happier and happier and happier and happier?

Take any quality you want in your story and push it. Not once, not twice, not three times, not four times... but seven to ten times. This gives you the kind of sustained action, sorrow, romance, comedy, etc. that truly makes a story come alive and glues the reader to their seat.

Plot We've Got, Quite A Lot

If you want to study plot—twist, turns, reversals of fortune—nothing is more revealing than the movie we mentioned earlier, *The Court Jester* with Danny Kaye. In the movie, the opening song declares: *"Plot we've got, quite a lot"* and they do!

Let's take a look (*The Court Jester* spoilers below!):

> The rightful king has been killed. A villain has taken the throne. In the forest, the Black Fox has rescued one member of the royal family, an infant. The Black Fox is gathering people to restore the child to the throne. One of those helping him is...an entertainer?

The entertainer, whose name is Hawkins, wants to be a daring knight—does he succeed?

No! Instead, he is given a boring task that he thinks should be done by a girl: the task of bringing the baby to an Abbey.

But, good news! He travels there with one of the Black Fox's captains, a competent and charming young woman named Maid Jean, whom the entertainer adores. Does he get there?

No! Something unexpectedly good happens. Maid Jean has feelings for him, too!

Even better, they meet a man on his way to the palace—a jester! An entertainer can be a jester, right? Maid Jean talks our Hawkins into knocking the jester on the head and impersonating him. Now, Hawkins can sneak into the palace and get the key to the secret passage, through which the Black Fox hopes to bring the troops he is amassing.

This Hawkins does, BUT unbeknownst to him, the jester he replaced is not actually a jester at all but a master assassin hired by a member of the court. Is this bad enough?

No! Maid Jean is captured by the king's men, who are

rounding up likely-looking young ladies for the king to pick for his companions. Now, instead of making it to the Abbey, the baby is hidden at the castle, too!

Is pretending to be a jester, who someone else thinks is an assassin, while trying to get the key to the tunnel bad enough?

No! The king wants the princess to marry the grim, gruesome, grisly Griswald. Only the princess's companion, a witch, has filled her head with tales of romance. When the princess threatens the life of the witch if the promised "true love" does not appear, the witch hypnotizes Hawkins, who, bedazzled and not recalling who he is, declares his love for the princess. Is this bad enough?

No! Who should the hypnotized Hawkins run into but Maid Jean, who has stolen the key from the king. She gives it to him, but, being hypnotized, he doesn't know why it is important, and the king gets it back.

Not only that, but Hawkins also speaks with the man who hired the assassin, who instructs him to kill the king's advisers.

And it goes on and on from there, with complication after complication being piled upon the head of our hapless Hawkins, who—through a mix of wits and sheer luck—manages to survive one outrageous turn of events, just in time to be confronted with another, even more outrageous one.

Note: Some of the unexpected turns go very badly for our hero. But some go well. The jester stumbles in where Hawkins and the captain are sheltering from the rain. The witch hypnotizes him into being an excellent swordsman right when the villain is trying to run him through. When his death by jousting seems certain, his armor is struck by lightning and becomes magnetized. This unexpected advantage saves his life.

And many more in like vein.

The Court Jester provides an excellent example of *what could make it more interesting?*—both better and worse—played out with charm and humor.

(This has nothing to do with plot, but this movie also contains one of the funniest bits of dialogue in any movie, when Hawkins learns that the toast cup for the joust has been poisoned and, *"the pellet with the poison's in the flagon with the dragon, and the vessel with the pestle has the brew that is true."* Truly a movie worthy of two hours of your time.)

Concept, Idea, and Two Strings

So how do you come up with a concept or idea intriguing enough to build a whole story around? The answer is *Two Strings*.

Two Strings, you may recall from Chapter Four, is the concept that your story needs two separate ideas to come alive. For instance, *mystery on a space station* crossed with *heating and cooling repairman who is always uncomfortable because no one calls him if their environment is pleasant.** A space station by itself is not necessarily interesting, but the unique take of the repair man adds dimension to the idea, similar to the way that contrast adds personality to characters.

One reason a story needs two strings is: As you are concocting your plots, thinking of worse and worse, or sadder and sadder, or more and more interesting occurrences, it can get strained or boring.

That's when you change strings.

Tired of thinking of air conditioning and heating problems? Have the space station be attacked! Tired of coming up with additional problems for the space station during the attack? Have the heating give out in a spectacular way, and now your space tech has to fix it while being shot at.

Can't think of another problem to throw between your hero and heroine? Switch back to your other string of the horse farm she lives on and have a horse throw a shoe or go into labor.

Etc., etc.

Notice how *The Court Jester* switched back and forth between the plotline involving Maid Jean trying to save the royal baby and the plotline involving the affairs of the castle —the false king, his daughter the princess, the man who hired the assassin, etc. Additional strings of plot make it easy to find specific, and unexpected, things that could get worse, or sadder, or more romantic, or funnier, etc.

Two strings is only the beginning. There is no limit to the number of strings you can weave into your work. But beware, you have to follow up on each one. Don't throw in more than you can handle. (The ideal number depends on the length of the work.)

And that, folks, is what makes plot tick.

*—I wrote that particular short story. It is called "Faces and Enigmas" and appears in my *In the Lamplight* anthology.

Exercise A: What could make it more interesting?

Take an event from your Work In Progress if you have one. If you don't, invent a possible turn of events for a character. Ask yourself:

What could make this turn of events worse for your character?
What else could make it worse—or more interesting?
What else could make it worse—or more interesting?
What else could make it worse—or more interesting?

Then ask this question again and again, until you have a list of seven to ten events. Write the answers down in a simple list form.

Bonus Exercise B:

Repeat Exercise 4A a couple more times. Alter worst with other qualities: *happier, sadder, tenser, more mysterious, more romantic,* etc.

Bonus Exercise C:

This is purely for fun. Combine the *what could make it more...* exercise with the Two Strings going-up-the-hill exercise. Start with getting in the car and going up the hill, add a second string AND make things worse... or better, or sadder, or happier, etc.

We got in the car.
   We drove up the hill.
   We reached the summit.

CHAPTER 9: INFODUMPS BEGONE!

Inserting Information: *Backstory that the reader longs for becomes revelation.*

Recently, a friend read my anthology, *In The Lamplight,* and commented that he noticed there were no infodumps. This took me by surprise because it was not something I had set out to do on purpose. But as I began to investigate, I realized what he meant.

The method I use for disseminating information so that it does not appear in a dump—or, worse, an infodumpster fire—is similar to the method used in the movie *Coco*. I will speak about that later.

Escaping the dreaded infodump comes down to the art of *placing exposition.*

Escaping Puddlehood

Once upon a time, I had to move a large chunk of exposition. It was stuck in the middle of a rather active scene and more than one reader had complained it was awkward and dull.

I realized it had to be moved. *But where?*

Ideally, I wanted it in a place where it would increase the readers' interest, rather than bore them. But how to find such a place? I thought it was fascinating, but readers thought it was in the middle of an otherwise tense scene and had to go. So it needed a new home. Yet, how could I tell when readers would agree with me, and when they would groan and pull out their hair?

In the end, I divided it into four pieces, putting each part into a place where it added to the scene rather than subtracting from it.

I wish I could tell you I did it gracefully.

But I can't. I dissolved into an emotional puddle.

When I recovered from puddlehood and buckled down to moving the scene, I had an insight that will, God willing, help others avoid a puddle-related fate in the future. It was about how to evaluate a passage to decide if a given piece of exposition would increase or decrease the reader's interest in a given location. This insight revolved around the Japanese girls' video game: *Long Live the Queen*.

Long Live Exposition

For those who have never played the game, Long Live the Queen is a text-based adventure. One plays an adorably cute fourteen-year-old princess named Elodie who must live to her 15th year in order to be crowned Queen.

Each turn of the game counts as one week of Elodie's life. Each week, the player chooses classes to attend in order to gain skills that Elodie needs to survive. There are 39 skills to choose from, varying from *Royal Deportment* to *Divination* to *Military Strategy* to *Falconry* to *Magic*. Each skill may be needed to negotiate through the various events Elodie must face if she wishes to survive.

The way the game is designed, it is impossible to learn all the skills. The key to reaching the coronation alive is to pick the correct skills needed to pass challenges that Elodie must face and to hone these skills to a high enough capacity. If she lacks enough expertise with the correct skills when a challenge arises, she *dies*.

Since learning skills is the difference between life and death, it is essential to learn as many as you can as quickly as possible. According to the game play mechanics, whether or not Elodie can learn a given skill slowly or rapidly depends upon her mood.

That's right—mood is the key to succeeding at this game!

There are eight moods (Angry, Afraid, Cheerful, Depressed, etc.) Some skills can be learned more quickly if Elodie is cheerful. Others will gain the same learning bonus if she is afraid. The activities she does in her free time—such as going to court or sneaking out of the castle—raise or lower these moods.

You, the player, must pick which activity to have her engage in so as to, hopefully, produce the mood you need to get a bonus for the skill you wish her to learn. If you pick the wrong activity, you can end up putting the princess into the wrong mood. This may mean that Elodie suddenly has a negative to how quickly she can learn a skill that she needs in order to pass the next challenge.

This severely reduces how quickly she can gain competency, which, in turn, lessens her chance of survival.

Between the activity phase and the classes phase of the game, comes the story. During these bits of text exposition, events happen. Friends visit. Commoners bring petitions. Nobles challenge her to a duel. Her country is invaded!

These events also raise or lower Elodie's moods. Sometimes, they include skill checks that our princess passes or fails depending on what skills she has gained. Occasionally, there are choices to make: Raise taxes? Lower them? Keep them the same? Does she execute her annoying magic-using aunt? Or let her live?

And when she fails the skill checks, sometimes, she dies.

By now, you are wondering: *What in the name of the Almighty does this have to do with writing?*

Here is the insight: Imagine you have written that wonderful description of your character's relationship with his grandmother that you find just fascinating. You really want to include this scene in your story, but you are not sure where to put it. Use the *Long Live the Queen* rating system to decide where it should go.

Look at your scene. Pick some possible spots in your story where the scene could go. Then rate each spot in your manuscript using the following guidelines:

If adding your exposition takes away from the prevailing mood of the scene–that is like the princess discovering she can't learn a skill she wants because her mood is wrong. Mark that spot as a –1.

If the exposition does nothing for the scene, this is similar to having your princess take a class in a skill that currently has no modifier. It's okay, but there's no particular gain. And we all understand how important it is for her to increase her skills before the next skill check—or she will eat the gift of chocolate without realizing that it is poisoned... and *die!*

We'll call that position a **0**.

If your exposition will change the mood of your character in a way that is beneficial to your story, mark that spot: **+1**

If your exposition will lead your character to act (similar to the princess making her skills check), mark that spot: **+2**

If your exposition will influence a choice your character must make, mark that spot: **+3**

Then, put your cherished exposition in the spot in your manuscript that achieves the highest *Long Live the Queen* rating.

The Grandmother of All Examples

Perhaps you are scratching your head and wondering what in the world all these numbers mean. For the sake of clarity, here is a series of examples.

Negative One:

There your character is, dangling from the edge of a cliff, being shot at by rabid robots who work for his mortal enemy, Sly McGoon, who is trying to steal his invention and his gal, and you have him stop to reminisce about an argument his brother once had with his grandmother.

This may not be the best time for this bit particular of backstory. Readers are on the edge of their seats, waiting to find out, *does he live or die?* Does he save Priscilla Prettypots? Does his invention make it to the Patent Office in one piece?

Ye gads, man! Nobody wants to pause for four plodding pages about some blithering conversation with some ancient biddy!

In fact, I dare, say, it would probably be lower than a –1.

Zero:

This time, the scene follows Priscilla Prettypots as she wanders through a mountain field picking the flowers she uses to make her pots pretty. As she picks flowers, Priscilla stops to reminisce about the time her brother had an argument with their grandmother. Then, she goes back to picking flowers, just as before.

Umm. Okay. That…happened, though we, the readers, have no idea why. It didn't exasperate us and make us want to pull out our hair, but it hasn't really done anything for us either.

It's over now. Moving on. Effect on us: **0**

Plus One:

This time, Priscilla is still walking among the flowers, but she's lonely. She's sad. Her beloved, Hugh Hardboiled, is hanging from a cliff somewhere, pursued by rabid robots, and there is nothing she can do to help. She sighs and clasps her hands over her heart. She may never see him alive again.

As she strolls, she reminisces about an argument her brother once had with her grandmother. The memory does not change her situation, Hugh is still hanging from a cliff, but it does cheer her, chase away her blues. While she arrived with a sad frown, she leaves with an armful of flowers, smiling.

The scene did not topple mountains—or save Hugh—but at least it affected something. Priscilla has stopped whining and now awaits, with a happy heart, the triumphant return of her beloved beau.

Or, if you prefer, Priscilla, ignorant of her beloved's fate, is singing cheerfully and picking flowers on the mountainside when she suddenly remembers that old argument between her brother and her grandmother. This reminiscence casts a shadow over her day. Her good mood evaporates, leaving her frowning and sad—making her all the more emotionally vulnerable when word reaches her of Hugh's horrible predicament.

Either way, in this position, the scene actually had an effect on the story because it has changed a character's mood. +1

Plus Two:

Priscilla is back in her mountainside cottage, filling her pretty pots with water to hold her flowers, when her brother stomps into her kitchen, spreading mud everywhere, and accidentally knocking over one of the pretty pots. The pot shatters.

Priscilla, staring in shock at the shards of the formerly pretty pot, recalls how her brother has always behaved in such a ramshackle manner. Why, was not this very behavior the cause of a famous argument between him and her beloved grandmother? Why hadn't their parents backed her grandmother that day? Maybe if they had been firmer with their eldest, he would not have grown up to be such a rapscallion.

Fueled by the anger the memory has provoked, Priscilla marches forward and slaps her brother across the face!

This time, the memory spurred the character to act: +2

Plus Three:

Alone on the mountainside, Priscilla paces back and forth, chewing on her fingernails. Hugh is in deadly danger, but she can do nothing! She desperately wants him to live, but she dare not approach the cliff side. What could she, a weaponless young woman, do against rabid robots? What if coming closer brings her within the grips of the dastardly Sly McGoon? She would only make Hugh's predicament worse!

Only, Priscilla, thinking back upon her childhood, recalls an argument between her brother and her grandmother. The argument had grown worse and worse, and Priscilla, afraid of being drawn into it, had begun to creep out of the room. Partway through the door, however, an idea had struck her.

It had taken great courage to turn around and interrupt the fearsome quarrel between her older brother and intimidating grandparent, but she had found the strength. To her delight, her solution had been joyfully accepted by both parties.

What if Priscilla could find the courage to march forward? What if she did have something to offer Hugh? What if her mere presence would be enough to make the difference between failure and success? Could she not, at the very least, drop rocks off the cliff top onto the heads of rabid robots?

By golly, she would not give up her darling Hugh without a fight!

This placement of the memory contributes to Priscilla making a decision that changes the outcome of the story. +3

Summing-up Long Live the Queen

Look for the place where your information or background scene will have the highest Long Live the Queen Rating.

And if you can't find a place to put it where it has an effect on a character? Then, it might be time to consider cutting it. Or to rewrite it to have more of an impact on your characters' immediate situation.

If you remember this simple rule and apply it when adding exposition, you may make it to your coronation—in the form of publication—without ever being poisoned by chocolates or even dissolving into a puddle, which is the best for everyone, especially your furniture.

Exposition Sum-up

Avoid Info dumps with the *Long Live the Queen* method.

+1 – changes character's mood, emotion, approach.

+2 – changes what character does—leads to action.

+3 – character must make a choice and the info affects this choice.

Backstory vs. Revelation

Have you ever watched Japanese anime? They are

almost all set up the same way. You are introduced to the show with some fast and fun episodes, often with lots of humor. These continue until you come to like the character and are engaged in his or her struggle. Then—and only then—the character's sad backstory is revealed. (Every single character in anime, except for one, has some kind of sad backstory.)

By this time, you are sitting on the edge of your seat, yearning to know every detail about your beloved characters. You truly want to understand what made them the dynamic people they are today.

Now imagine the series had started with that background information—making you wade through some long boring story about the childhood of a character you care nothing about before you could get to the humor and the action. Would you have enjoyed that?

No, not at all.

And that, my fellow writers, is the difference between *revelation* and *backstory*.

Backstory is information you tell the reader about what happened before the present day of the story.

Revelation is the exact same information, once the reader *wants* to read about it.

The *Long Live the Queen* system can also be applied to backstory/revelation—a good revelation scene should be put at a point where the character needs to take an action or make a choice based upon something from the character's past.

The Elegance that is *Coco*

An excellent example of backstory and exposition done well is the movie *Coco*. I don't want to say too much for those who haven't seen it, but I recommend watching it and noticing how the situation and backstory come onstage. Note what you think is going on at different times in the movie. How were the various twists and turns set up? What clued you into each revelation?

This movie puts its exposition and revelations onstage with such elegance. It really is worth studying! And it is an enjoyable movie, too!

Exercise A: Long Live Your Story!

Look through your work in progress for three places where you reveal information or backstory. Rate the spots on the *Long Live the Queen* scale.

Does the information fit the mood of the scene?
Does it change the mood for the better?
Does it lead to action?
Does it lead to a character making a choice?

Can you find a way to increase the rating? For instance, can you introduce bits about your history at a time when it matters more to one of the characters?

CHAPTER 10: WOW, THAT WAS SATISFYING!

Satisfying Endings: *Tie the beginning and the end together—balance satisfaction and surprise.*

The End of Things

Have you ever read a book that started with a bang but ended with a whimper? The hook was great. The plot sucked you in. You loved the characters. And then...

Nada.

Endings are almost as important as beginnings. If the beginning is weak, they won't read your book. But if your ending is weak, they won't read your next one. That may not be a problem for that occasional author who only wishes to write one book. But it sure is a problem for the rest of us!

So how do we do it: write an ending that leaves the readers not regretting the time they invested in the story we have spun? The key is to balance the two factors that we all yearn for in an ending: *satisfaction* and *surprise*.

Satisfying and surprising. Too much of the first and the book is predictable, boring. Too much of the second, and the story is unsatisfying. So how do we get an ending that is surprising and yet still satisfying?

There are many answers, but here are two helpful ideas.

Satisfying

Satisfying: the secret is to weave beginnings and endings together.

Have you ever read a column by humorist Dave Barry? He has a formula that he has used for years. He starts his columns with subject A. He meanders into subject B. Then, at the end, he suddenly brings up subject A again, tying A and B together.

The result is almost always very satisfying (and often quite funny, but I digress.)

I recommend you look Mr. Barry's columns up online.

Dave Barry Endings

As fiction writers, we can do this, too. When you get to the end of your story, go back and look at the beginning—the first chapter or two. Read it though again. Note what subjects you touch on. Then look over your last chapter or two.

Look for things you introduced early on that you can touch on in your last chapter or so. Look for things you mention in your end game that you could introduce right at the beginning.

Does the dog save the day? Can you mention the dog in Scene One? Does the hero stop to enjoy a sunset in the opening chapters? Can you show his reaction to a sunset in one of the last few scenes, showing the distance he has come by noting how his reaction to the sunset is the same and how it is now different?

Follow up on threads. Notice ideas you introduced. Did you touch on them again in the middle? Can you refer to them again at the end? Perhaps mentioning how the character has changed? All this leads to a satisfying reading experience.

A note for people writing serials. Many of us have threads that span multiple volumes. If you introduce a thread in one book and it will not be resolved until another book, make sure you return to it at the end of the first volume—so the reader knows that not tying up this thread is deliberate. Otherwise, the readers will assume that you, the author, forgot, and the story will feel unfinished and unsatisfying.

It can be really quick: *and we still did not know who had stolen the painting.* Or: *Roger had failed to find the dragon today, but there was still tomorrow.* Even the shortest mention will do wonders—to keep the readers from feeling as if they are suddenly standing on thin air.

An Example of Satisfying:

An example from a writing assignment submitted by author Paul Go illustrates this:

From Chapter 1:

He pulled a hangman's noose and nearly vomited as his X35 executed his commands. Even with the inertial dampers, he was shaken within the cockpit.

"Wish I had an inertial belt," he muttered as he completed the maneuver.

From Chapter 27:

Hornet flew through space, the ship he piloted falling behind him rapidly. He had launched from the open cockpit just like Starstruck had suggested.

"Brilliant idea, greenhorn. Now you have to catch me. At this speed, I'll be like a fly on a windscreen."

He saw the DoubleStar ahead, its rear hatch open. In it stood Starstruck, holding something in his hand. He threw it at Hornet who slowed almost immediately as the thing came in close enough to grab.

"Well I'll be, greenhorn. An inertial belt. Nice thinking."

He came in and was easily caught by Starstruck. He looked at his rescuer and smiled. There were no words.

In addition to having major issues echoed from the beginning to the end, it can be very satisfying for readers if minor issues are revisited near the end. It rewards the readers for the effort they put into the work and makes it feel as if every word counts.

Surprising

Surprising: The secret is to set up clues that support the real conclusion.

Clues are pieces of information that appear to be unrelated to what they will eventually support. If clues are set to support the real ending along the way, the conclusion can be a surprise—not the ending that seemed predicted by events—and yet feel entirely supported by the story. A few thoughts on clue placements and applying this to endings.

Hiding Clues in a List

One excellent way to hide a clue is to list it in among other like things. In a list, always put the clue second when there are two options and in the middle when there are three or more options. This is particularly helpful if the information is being shared in a description, where you wish to include the needed information but not to draw attention to it.

Example: let's say that *lavender* is the clue you wish to place. Perhaps, lavender has a magical effect in your story, and the fact that it is present is going to turn out to be noteworthy at the end of the story. You want it mentioned, but you don't want to draw the readers' attention.

Two options list: Mint and lavender grew in the garden.

Three options list: She made a salad, throwing in dill, lavender buds, and basil.

Readers may notice the first thing listed. They might possibly later recall the last thing in a list, but readers almost never pay much attention to the middle of a list.

Drawing the Wrong Conclusion

When planting clues, many authors make a particularly exasperating mistake. They put clues onstage, but they don't want the reader to draw the correct conclusion. So they have their characters ignore the clues.

This drives readers batty. Sharp readers notice the clues. They draw the correct conclusion. The fact that the characters fail to do so, particularly if they continue to do so over time, begins to annoy the readers, who soon begins to pin their annoyance on the last person you want them to blame: *the author—you.*

If your characters have encountered the necessary clues, even if it is early in the story, let them make the correct deduction—then take it from there. There are many ways to handle having true information come onstage.

The characters can figure out only part of the truth. They can figure out this leg of the truth, but encounter a new obstacle—a new missing piece of information that is now needed. Or—and this is particularly useful when setting up surprising endings—they can review the clues, deduce the real answer, discard that answer for some seemingly good reason, and *draw a false conclusion.*

This way, you avoid the trap of having the reader see a twist coming a mile away and be frustrated with the character for his pigheadedness, and you set up a revelation that can be revisited, and discovered to be true after all, during the story's climax.

Example: Upon seeing Sarah's car at Tom's house, your character correctly deduces that Sarah must have been at Tom's the night of the dragon sighting. But then something convinces your character otherwise.

Perhaps she overheard Peter say he had borrowed Sarah's car and thinks that Peter was there instead, not realizing that Peter had returned the car before noon.

Perhaps she sees that the milkman drives a car very similar to Sarah's and now assumes the car at Tom's belonged to someone other than Sarah—perhaps even the milkman.

Perhaps she confronts Sarah early on, and Sarah admits she was there but claims that she fell asleep waiting for Tom to finish his video game and missed all the action.

In each of these scenarios, you have now established that Sarah's car was at Tom's—a fact you can use for your surprising conclusion—but you have also dismissed from the mind of the character, and, thus, most likely, from the mind of the reader, that Sarah was present during the important event. This is highly preferable to mentioning a car that looks like Sarah's car early on and then never having the character conclude that it might be Sarah's while the reader, who has noticed the resemblance stews, or worse, puts the book down.

Misdirection Is Your Friend

Try to put necessary supporting information for your surprising big reveal into the story in such a way that it does not seem to be related to where you are going with it. An easy way to do this is: Think of a thing, think of the side effects of that thing, and put the side effects onstage without saying why they are there.

Example: If the villain is secretly trying to go to the moon, have the hero discover solid rocket booster fuel hidden in a cabinet in the villain's lair without any indication of what the villain planned to do with it. When the villain's massive rocket comes onstage in the final scene, the reader will be surprised, and then, they will think: *Oh, of course! That's what the rocket fuel was for! This has been set up all along!*

If the hero can draw the wrong conclusion—perhaps he fears the villain wants to turn the fuel into a weapon—that is even better.

Lavender Dilly-Dilly

134 | THE ART AND CRAFT OF WRITING

Below is an example from *The Awful Truth about Forgetting*. It is a simple example, but it will do:

Clue One—placed in the first three chapters:
The main characters are approaching a warded facility. As they pass through a number of types of wards, they chat about them, including how fresh baked bread is useful for warding off magical beasts:

"**Lavender's good for warding off magical beasts, too,**" murmured Rachel, gazing hungrily at the bread. Then she felt a bit foolish. Feeling tempted by magical creature bait hardly redounded to her greater glory.

"Lavender?" asked both the boys.

Rachel nodded. "No animals eat it, nor bugs either. The plant, that is. Bees and butterflies eat the flowers, of course. And unicorns, but they are hardly a problem. **That's why lavender is the prime ingredient in Bogey Away.**"

Clue Two—about half-way through the book, during a chapter about the celebration of Yule:

After that, an entire day was spent wrapping presents and addressing cards. Rachel posted the Yule cards she had drawn, along with hand-picked presents for her closest friends. For those she knew less well ... she included perfume, soap, or candles from the Gryphon Park Lavender Farm .... While at the farm's lavender shop, **she also picked up a handful of bottles of the Bogey Away spray** she had described at Ouroboros Industries to send to William and Gaius.

. . .

Clue Three—at the start of a long scene on the ice that leads to the climax of the story:

Rachel patted her coat and robes, searching for something she could give as a gift. ... In the pocket of her red wool coat, she found some lavender lip balm, **two bottles of Bogey Away left from Yule,** and a blue origami crane that she had made that morning with her mother's gift paper.

Resolution—near the end of the book, when Rachel and Astrid—still on skates—are being tormented by pixies in the dark:

"What would we do at home?" she murmured, her voice warbling. Then, suddenly, she laughed, "Silly me."

"Silly... Why?" Astrid's gentle voice was tinged with hope. "You know what to do?"

Reaching into her coat pocket, Rachel pulled out the two small bottles left in her pockets from the Yule holiday and put one into Astrid's hand. "Here. Spray them."

The *swish* of spray bottle pumps sounded in the darkness.

"*Och! I am slain!*" cried Sir Thistlewhip, though he sounded perfectly hale.

"*Flee, flee!*" cried Sir Rosethorn, "*before the putrid miasma bears down the rest of us!*"

"*But what of the delicacies!*" inquired Sir Eglantine. "*The strapping giantesses?*"

"*Flee! Flee, I say!*"

With buzzing and high, sweet cries of knightly woe, the pixies fled into the snowy night.

"And good riddance!" Astrid shouted into the darkness. Then, she grew quiet and ducked her head, as if startled by her own show of pluck. After a moment, however, she sniffed the cold air. "Smells like…" she breathed more deeply, "lavender?"

"Lavender is useful for many things," Rachel replied gaily, giving the little bottle of Bogey Away an extra squirt before she returned it to her pocket.

Notice that at no point in the novel did Rachel Griffin think: *Gee, I might be attacked by pixies, so I should get a bottle of Bogey Away and carry it around at all times.* That would have been too obvious. The first mention was sparked by the environment—the discussion of different kinds of wards. The second was a reaction to the first—she wanted to show the young men she had been talking with the Bogey-Away. The third was chance, slipped in among many things when she was looking through her pockets for a gift she could give someone.

When she finally uses the Bogey-Away to chase away the pixies, it is hopefully a bit surprising to a reader of the novel, for whom these clues came spaced quite far apart, but also satisfying, because a subject introduced early in the book turned out to be useful at the end.

The more unrelated the mentions of the clues are to the final use of them, the more surprising the resolution is—and yet, if well-placed, they will lead to an ending that will not have the *out of the blue* sensation that would otherwise make it feel abrupt and unsatisfying.

This concludes our subject. Now is your chance to plant those threads and weave them together to satisfy your reader!

Exercise A: An Ending that Satisfies

Tie the beginning of your story to the end.

Find a thread or issue that exists in the beginning of your story.

Echo that idea at the end.

Or find an idea or theme that is clear at the end of the story, and echo that idea in a scene, description, or conversation near the beginning.

Example: Chekov's Gun. If you use a gun in the climax, remember to mention it lying on the mantelpiece early on. Conversely, if you mention that there is a gun in a room in an early description, use it in the climax. Remember, this is not limited to guns. It can apply to anything: cups, cats, hats, whatever is needed in the climax can have a cameo in the early pages and vice versa.

Try to have at least three things echoed between the opening and the closing. The more things you can wrap up or come back to at the end, the more satisfying the story.

Exercise B: Side Effects as Clues

Think about the events of your plot. Think about side effects of the actions of the adversaries or other actors in the story.

Look for places where you can add these side effects in as clues that will, ultimately, support your climax.

Exercise C: Clue Placement

Look through your story for any place where your character makes a decision or figures something out. Can you add facts or events earlier in the story to support this decision/deduction? If so, those are the "clues."

Look for places in the story to put these supporting clues, in such a way that the information is onstage for the reader, even if not it is obvious why the information is important. Look for ways to make the information blend into the background so that it does not attract too much attention when it first comes onstage.

Try to find at least three places where you can add or enhance a clue to better support a later decision or climatic event.

The more aspects of the ending you can set up without the reader realizing where you are heading, the more surprising it will be—without seeming random.

PART THREE: THE ART OF WRITING

CHAPTER 11: HEART AND SOUL

Conveying Emotion: *Add visceral reactions—physical involuntary reactions—to heighten the connection with the reader.*

We have gripping descriptions. We have living, breathing characters. We have quite a lot of plot. How do we pull it all together to make our readers burn with the bliss and suffer the sorrow of... well, our characters and plot?

Remember the idea that if you want the reader to care, the character has to care? It has a corollary. If you want Readers to feel, the character has to show them what to feel. Without the hints as to the character's emotional reactions, we, the readers, don't know what emotion we are supposed to experience when an event occurs.

So how do we do this?

Society for the Preservation of the Adverb

The simplest way to express what a character's emotion

is just to say it, and the easiest way to say in a dialogue tag with an adverb.

"Hello!" he said *jauntily.*

"Goodbye," she said *glumly.*

Pick up almost any older children's book, *Winnie the Pooh*, *Ramona the Pest,* and you will find them filled with descriptive terms and adverbs. Why? Because children's authors understand that children want to know. Simply, clearly, they want to know how the speaker is speaking. This matters to children. Is he angry? Is she happy?

It matters to many adult readers, too.

Now, it is likely that every single other writing source you ever come upon will tell you not to do this. Not me. I *love* adverbs. They add spice. I am, in fact, a charter member of the Society for the Preservation of the Adverb.

I also love words for speaking that are not "said."

"Hello," he *chuckled.*

"Goodbye," she *hissed.*

When I was a kid, I loved the author Anne McCaffery. I remember pouring through her *Dragonsriders of Pern* series and counting how many words she used in place of "said" in one book: *he laughed, she smiled, he grinned, she chortled,* etc. I counted 22 such words.

I cannot express the admiration I felt, as a teenager, for this author who was able to come up with 22 words for *said*, and I loved her books. I still love those books. I still admire her use of descriptive vocal words.

The idea that you should not use adverbs or alternate words for *said* was pioneered by Hemingway and made popular by some of the noir mystery writers. This was partially because both adverbs and these alternate words for *said*, were, at one time, overused. So it was new and chic to not use them. But they were overused nearly a century ago.

Most people today have never read the works that made people shy away from them.

Yes, they can be overused. Yes, many beginners overuse them. But telling authors not to use them because they might overuse them is like telling a chef not to use salt because some beginners pour in too much.

I have a brief funny story on this subject. When my *Prospero's Children* series was slated to be published by Tor, my editor tried to talk me out of using adverbs and what he called *said bookisms*. (Apparently, once upon a time, there were "Said books" that had lists of other words you could use instead of said.)

I responded that I thought such language was appropriate for the type of fantasy I was writing. They added color.

He said, *"If you put them in, your books won't sell."*

I countered, *"But one of my favorite writers uses them all the time."*

He replied, *"I bet their books don't sell well. What's the author's name?"*

I responded: *"J. K. Rowling."*

He let me keep them.

The Myth of Tagless Dialogue

Now, that we have defended the honor of these spice-like words, it is important to use them sparingly. Like spices, a little makes the food much tastier, a lot can ruin it entirely. You don't want adverbs accompanying every line of dialogue, but one does not need to avoid them entirely—they are a very quick way to convey a lot of information about mood and emotion to the reader.

Let us pause and explore the myth that you don't need to

indicate emotion in dialogue. "All you need to do is be skilled enough at writing dialogue to indicate the emotion." This idea came from authors who wrote noir-style stories... where every single character is cynical at all times.

That system breaks down very quickly when your characters start exhibiting a wider range of human emotions or when you wish to portray a character who doesn't always say what he means.

A good example is Mephistopheles Prospero, again from *Prospero's Children*. Note the difference between these three sentences:

"Everyone in my family is an idiot," he said.

"Everyone in my family is an idiot." He threw up his hands and twirled in a circle.

"Everyone in my family is an idiot," he chirped cheerfully, throwing up his hands and twirling in a circle.

Anyone who came away with the same image from reading the first sentence that they did from the last one can drop out now. You do not need adverbs.

For the rest of us, could you tell from the first example that Mephisto was cheerful? That his words belied his mood? Or did you hear in your head something much more like:

"Everyone is my family is an idiot," he grumbled.

Sentence two might have given the impression of

someone speaking lightly, or, it might have caused readers to scratch their heads and think, "Wha...huh? Why is his twirling? This writer makes no sense."

Sentence three, however, is perfectly clear. The speaker's words are at odds with his lighthearted, cheerful attitude.

When writing characters who are subtle or complex, we cannot rely on mere words to properly communicate emotions. Spice-words, such as adverbs and synonyms for *said* can help close that gap.

But what if you want something a bit more subtle? Remember, we don't want our meal of words to get too spicy.

How Do We Perceive Emotion?

You walk into your house. Two family members are talking loudly in the hallway. How, other than listening to what they are saying, do you tell whether they are joyful or angry?

The answer: We look at their facial expressions. We listen to their tone of voice. We note their body language. Are they laughing and smiling, or standing tensely and scowling? Are they leaning on the door jamb and gesturing openly? Or have they curled their hands into to fists so tightly that their knuckles are white?

These are the things that tell us in real life what people's emotions are. As writers, our job is to convey this information to the reader. By describing these same signals to the reader, we can convey emotions more subtly than by merely declaring *she said happily* or *he cried angrily*.

As we discussed in the chapter on descriptions that the reader is like a person in a virtual reality experience. You, the author, are providing the input. You can provide direct

146 | THE ART AND CRAFT OF WRITING

input such as: *he grumbled,* and subtler input such as *his shoulders were hunched, and he would not look her in the eye.*

But there is a very special kind of virtual input that authors can give their readers that is even more effective than descriptions of emotional cues.

Pretty in Pink

Margie Lawson is a psychologist who works as a therapist, so she really gets to see people express the full range of human emotions. At work, Margie notices the physical actions and gestures that accompany strong emotional reactions. She also teaches writing courses. In her courses, she shares these observations with her students.

The classes are great fun, and the alumni include many published writers. A number of Margie's previous students have gone on to hit the Bestseller's List. So, she knows of what she teaches.

One of the great revelations that Margie shares is the power of including the POV character's *visceral reactions.* In her EDITS system, she assigns colors to certain aspects of writing to help authors track what they are and are not including in their manuscript. The color assigned to visceral reactions is pink.

By visceral reactions, we mean involuntary responses. "Her breath caught in her throat." "Her heart hammered like a hungry woodpecker." "Her knees knocked together." "She swallowed." These are the involuntary reactions we all have to moments of heightened emotion: sudden happiness, fear, terror, sad news, etc.

They are the ways we feel these high emotion moments in our body.

A POV (point of view) character's visceral reaction has a

different effect on the reader than the reaction of some other character. The reader associates with the POV character (in a good book, anyway). So when the POV reports that her heart skipped a beat, or his head throbbed, we *feel* this...and it helps lock down the related emotion in our imaginations.

Now, you may ask: *Why is this important?*

As readers, we assume that emotional reactions are a given. We read. Stuff is on the page. We react to it. Right?

Not exactly. Some authors have been taught that they should just say what happened and leave the rest up to the reader. But if the author does not indicate to the reader what reaction is expected, the reader often has the wrong reaction.

A brief example:

The giant spider climbed over the wall. Eight enormous eyes glinted in the moonlight.

Filbo's heart grew cold in his chest. He pressed a hand against his throat. If Perry and Mippin had not been waiting on the far side, relying upon him, he would have turned back then and there.

The giant spider climbed over the wall. Eight enormous eyes glinted in the moonlight.

"This'll be a cinch!" Indiana Dundee laughed in his charming accent. His grin widened as he felt that heady rush of adrenaline that accompanied the hunt. "For Arachne Gigantua, we recommend a size seven net."

The giant spider climbed over the wall. Eight enormous eyes glinted in the moonlight.

Tears welled up in Sarah's eyes, "Oh Arachne! You're okay! You lived!"

Beginning writers often believe that the description of the spider is enough to inspire fear. But people can have a myriad of reactions to any event. If your main character does not react with fear to what was happening, neither will your reader.

(This is not to say that an author cannot write a scene where the POV is not scared, but the reader is… but that takes more finesse. Often, secondary characters are then used to indicate fear, so that the main character seems foolhardy or brave, etc. in contrast to the "ordinary people" around him. We see this often in anime and TV shows, where secondary characters have exaggerated reactions that help the audience understand the courage of the main character.)

What Margie's *Empowering Character's Emotion* class brings out is that the number-one, most effective way to communicate emotional reactions to the reader is through the visceral reaction of the point of view character. When we read these involuntary responses, we tend to experience them, too… and we associate them in our minds with certain emotions.

If we read that a character had butterflies in his stomach, we often feel a momentarily ghostly flutter ourselves, as we remember what that is like. We remember moments when we were in front of a crowd or had to make a confession. Those subconscious associations with the visceral reaction get channeled into our reaction to the scene in the book. It makes it that much more vivid, that much more real.

One does not want a lot of pink in one's manuscript. Too much, and it stops having the desired effect. The reader pulls away. It's like the difference between the shock when a quiet person yells once or what happens when a loud person yells a lot. The quiet person gets our attention. The loud people are soon tuned out. (Take it from a mom.)

Too much pink, as Marie Lawson calls it, and the reader balks. Not enough and they do not engage. Just right and all your food will be eaten by Goldilocks... er, I mean, and the reader will have a vivid and enjoyable experience reading your book.

So, what we want is little dabs of pink here and there—just enough to keep readers engaged and on the edge of their seats.

One last point on this topic, many wise authors stress that the effective order of description is: stimulus/reaction; however, what they mean by this is confusing, as they use these terms in a strange way. So let's make it simpler by saying visceral reaction/mental reaction.

You want to tell the readers what the visceral reaction is and then tell us why the character experienced it. *He flinched back. There was a giant spider hanging in the room.* Or, *Her eyes filled with tears. She would never see her beloved teddy bear again.* First the visceral reaction and then the mental reaction, the reason why the character is having this reaction.

And now, I breathe a *huge sigh of relief* as we come to the end. (Notice the pink!)

For anyone who is interested in learning more, Margie Lawson's classes can be found at margielawson.com. She offers classes online, or her lectures can be purchased directly.

Exercise A: Add Emotion!

Go through your story. Pick a few description or action scenes. Add hints and reactions from characters in the scene to help the reader know what emotion they are supposed to be feeling.

Find at least three places you can enhance your story in this fashion.

Feeling bold? Take the same scene and rewrite it so as to evoke a different emotional reaction. (If you want the reader to be frightened, try for humor. To be angry, try for sad, etc.)

Don't put the second version in your story, but you may learn something interesting.

Exercise B: Adding Pink

Go through your Work In Progress and find three places where you can add a visceral reaction to the Point of View character. Can he *gasp, stumble, feel weak kneed, clench his fists, grit his teeth, feel the prick of tears*? Can she *sigh, blink, flinch, clench her stomach, curl her toes reflexively*? (You don't have to actually make the text pink—though you may, if you wish.)

Find three places where "pink" will improve your story.

Ideal spots are any place you want the reader to have a strong emotional reaction. The more dramatic the scene, the more benefit from a bit of "pink." If you don't have a work-in-progress, just write three short paragraphs where a POV character experiences a visceral reaction.

Remember to have the visceral reaction first, followed by the character's mental thoughts or the narrator showing the reason for this reaction.

CHAPTER 12: INTERIOR DIALOGUE

Interior Dialogue: *Readers don't trust dialogue. Let your characters think, and let what they think be juxtaposed to the dialogue, showing the readers a new angle.*

This one I learned the hard way.

When I first started writing novels, I was under the impression that the best writing was like a screenplay, all dialogue—everything out in the open. So I set out to write just that. I put everything into dialogue. I would figure out what the character wanted or was thinking. Then, I would find a way to have him speak this thought aloud.

Back then, I had two friends reading my work—the same two who set me right about adding senses to descriptions. When I finished a chapter, I would send it to them, and, invariably, they would write back and ask (along with a request for more sense impressions), *"What is your main character thinking?"*

To which, I would stare at the page in absolute puzzlement and then, *gesturing at it wildly*, cry out, "But I just told you what he was thinking! He said it *out loud!*"

Then, one day, it struck me. *They did not believe him.*

No matter what I had the character say, unless I did something to indicate in the text what his opinion was—unless I showed them his thoughts—they did not know if he was telling them the truth.

They did not know if his happiness was true or feigned. They did not know if he agreed with his words or was just saying them to be polite. They did not know if he actually liked the guy he was talking to or was secretly wishing the bloke would take a long walk off a short pier.

No matter how much of his heart the character poured into his dialogue, it never occurred to them that this was also what he was thinking.

To Scriptwrite or Not to Scriptwrite

Modern writers are often led astray by television and movies. They have scripts, right? They just speak out loud with very few voiceovers, right? So we can do that in a book, right?

Wrong.

The part played by inner dialogue in a novel is provided by facial expressions with movies and TV—by the acting. Did the character grimace when he said that? Did he roll his eyes? Is her face suffused with joy? Those are the things that fill in the rest of the story for us, that tell us what the character is feeling, and—most importantly—that tell us what we, the audience, should feel.

Internal thoughts are another form of "string' that can be used—another chance for an author to show contrast in the story. In this case, the contrast is between what is being said and what is being thought. (In fact, it could be argued that inner thoughts are the best secondary string. It is inner thoughts that give us the character's motives.)

And, as we all recall, contrast is what brings out three-dimensionality.

Adding contrast does not mean that what a character is thinking always has to be the opposite of what he says. Characters don't all have to be pathological liars. Some characters say what they mean—but very few characters, even the most honest—say *everything* they mean.. Showing the character's thinking gives the author a chance to add details, nuances—shading.

Is the character worried about what he is saying? Is she excited for a reason she has not yet put into words? Is he tired, so that his main attention is not on his dialogue, but on how quickly he can get home and relax. Is she actually thinking about cheese? Or chocolate?

Does he have a hidden agenda?

(Hidden agendas do not need to be bad things—picture a character trying to subtly discover a friend's schedule so she can plan a surprise birthday party.)

Finally, inner thoughts can be a good vehicle for putting across information no one would bother saying in words: how long people have known each other, where the character's watch came from, tidbits of background information about the setting, that sort of thing.

How We Show Our Inner Landscape

Internal thoughts and feelings can be indicated in two ways. The first is to put the thoughts on stage directly:

. . .

Example 1) *She loved the old couch. It pained her to see it in such bad shape.*

Or, even:

Example 2) *She thought: I love that old couch. How sad that they let it get like this.*

The second is to show without telling:

Example 3) *She ran her hand slowly over the old couch, stroking its worn upholstery and running her finger along the crack in the polished wood of the arm.*

Or, show with some tell.

Example 4) *She ran her hand slowly over the old, worn couch, sad to see it in such a state of disrepair.*

Which method is better? Whichever one fits the story.

Though often just a bit of tell helps a whole lot. When it is all show, sometimes readers miss what the author wished to convey. As we saw in the previous chapter when discussing conveying emotions, not all readers pick up the same emotional cues from action alone. Thus many authors use a mix.

The second example above is probably the least common. Direct thoughts in conversation form are rare. Often, if thoughts appear in such a straightforward form, it is to emphasize irony.

Modern writing books push the third: showing with no telling. Showing is great for two reasons. One, you often have a chance to use either visceral reactions or sense impressions, both things that can make the story more vivid for the reader. Two, when you convey by showing, it is similar to how we, in real life, figure out what other people are feeling—by seeing their expression, how they move, and what they do.

Sometimes this show-only method works. I think it's relatively clear in my example above what is going on. As a reader, however, I find sometimes this method does not work. As I mentioned above, not every reader has the same expectation of what a certain gesture or action means.

If the reader's expectations don't match those of the author, the reader is left scratching their head and saying, "Huh?"

Many readers can list specific authors whose works leave them feeling this way. Sometimes, they cannot tell at all what a character's reaction is supposed to convey. The internal thought responsible for the motivation of the character did not communicate itself in the scene.

If the woman's emotional reaction to the couch was important to either the plot or character development, one might go with:

She ran her hand slowly over the old couch, stroking its worn upholstery and running her finger along the crack in the polished wood of the arm. She loved the old couch. It pained her to see it in such bad shape.

If the matter were of very little importance, I would

recommend something more like Example Four. I would not, myself, use Example Two above on something as unimportant as a couch, unless I were writing *The Haunted Sofa, A Gothic for our Time*, and her direct thoughts were being overhead by the mind-reading entity dwelling in the old couch.

Or, if it was THE AMAZING SOFA!*

When done right, Internal Dialogue gives the reader a deeper sense of three-dimensionality and depth, hopefully, without weighing the story down.

Some of us learned this the hard way. Maybe, just maybe, you won't have to.

*The AMAZING SOFA—a superhero invented by my youngest son, part of a team of valiant superheroes known as the Justice Vigilantes for Justice!

Exercise A: Internal dialogue

Look for scenes in your story that are relatively straightforward and add internal dialogue. Make sure the internal dialogue shares information that is different from (or the opposite of) what is going on in the action and dialogue, thus providing a contrasting string to the scene.

Exercise B:

Try the above at least three times.

Exercise C:

See if you can get The Trick in there, too (i.e., if the internal dialogue shows us a change in emotions from happy to sad, sad to happy, angry to chagrinned, etc.)

CHAPTER 13: PAYLOAD MOMENTS

Payload Moments: Every scene should have a moment that moves the plot along or heightens awareness, drawing the reader into something greater.

What is a payload moment, you ask? It is the moment when the readers receive their payoff for the effort they have put into reading the story. A moment that reveals something they really want to know or broadens the horizons of the current canvas, hinting at something greater than they had been expecting.

They are the moments that make reading the story worthwhile.

When you sit down to write a payload moment, what you have to ask yourself is: *What can go in this scene that will take what has already been established and raise it to a higher level?*

What action, revelation, or interpretation will make the reader go, *"ah!"* or, *"oh, of course!"* or even, *"oh, no!"*

The payload moment is the moment lazy writers leave

out. If you read a book and its premise is interesting but the actual story is merely okay, *meh*, it is probably short on payload moments.

Types of Payloads

Payload falls into two categories: *scene payload* and *character payload*.

Scene Payload is the moment in the scene that delivers a payload moment: a revelation, an answer to a plot question, a new way of looking at the situation, a glimpse of something greater, something beyond the current experience.

Character Payload is usually revelation—motives, secrets, that sort of thing. The secret reasons behind what the character is doing. The true motive that is pushing them to act as they act. If you suddenly discover that the villain is committing his heinous acts because the man the hero killed in Chapter One was the villain's father—that is a character payload moment.

Wanted: Payload Moments

Every short story needs at least one payload moment... something that turns a premise on its head and gives the reader a new appreciation of what is being told.

Every novel should have a small payload moment in every chapter or major scene—the thing that makes the scene come alive and drive the reader to keep going—tying the current scene into the ongoing plot or even into the very nature of the universe itself. It should also have at least one major payload moment in the novel as a whole.

This is also true of fight scenes and sex scenes. Each one should have some moment that lifts the reader out of the immediate scene for just a moment, something that moves the plot along or heightens awareness, drawing the reader into something greater. Villains should reveal something important during a fight, and romantic partners should learn more about each other or reveal secrets during intimate moments.

Ideally, every character should have at least one paragraph/scene where he reveals his inner motivation.

Revelation of motive makes a great payload moment. That is an example of a kind of character payload.

Greater things? What's that?

Sometimes the payload moment is caused by the revelation of unexpected turns of the plot. Other times, it happens because the ideas in the story are suddenly revealed to be on a deeper or higher level than it had previously touched.

Here is an example:

There is a scene in a Japanese anime called *One Piece* where the main character, a pirate boy named Monkey D. Luffy, is about to be executed by a rival.

At the very last minute, as the curved blade lowers to strike off the head the poor imprisoned lad, the rival swinging the weapon is struck by lightning. A grizzled, cynical navy captain named Smoker, who was in a position to watch these proceedings, is seriously impressed both by the unexpected timing of the lightning bolt and by the fact that despite being about to lose his head, the pirate boy was smiling.

Captain Smoker, observing the scene, became convinced that *destiny* itself wanted this young man to live.

What was so impressive about this scene was that destiny had not been mentioned previously in this series, and this scene takes place in Episode 52. By observing the events in this way, Captain Smoker raises the interest and importance of the scene. He introduces the idea that Luffy is not a random pirate, but someone in whom destiny itself has an interest.

This changes the viewer's perspective of not only the scene of the attempted execution but also the entire series. Adding this question—whether Providence might be on the main character's side—adds a new dimension. The whole story suddenly seems deeper, wider, more important than it did previously.

That was a payload moment, not only for that episode, but for the entire first two seasons of *One Piece.*

Payload Moments Bring the Story to Life

The payload moment is the thing that makes the scene really come alive, that makes you sit up and exclaim, *"Wow."* It intensifies the story or deepens it. It can be something related to the greater universe, like learning that destiny is on your side, or it can be a twist of the plot—a new revelation about the situation that gives answers to plot questions or reveals secrets.

The best Payload moments are like a *zing*, a tiny jolt, the kind of shock you get when you touch a metal doorknob after walking on a carpet.

You sit up and open your eyes wider and exclaim, *"Wow!"*

Five Scenes with a Zing

There is a movie where the payload moments are so powerful that they fell like the thunderous retort of a full-strength lightning bolt. The movie is *The Five People You Meet In Heaven*. If you have not watched this movie, you might want to before you continue.

Spoiler Alert

The Five People You Meet in Heaven proposes the idea that when you die, but before you get to go on to Heaven, you meet five people who show you what your life really meant, who explain the mysteries you never understood while you were alive.

The particular story of the movie is about an amusement park maintenance man named Eddie who has lived and worked at this park his entire life, except for a stint in WWII. He had had plans, dreams, but when he came back from the war with his leg permanently damaged, those dreams slipped away from him. He took over his father's job at Ruby Pier, an amusement park that is a bit like New York's Coney Island, and never found the courage to break free.

Eddie dies trying to save a little girl from a damaged ride, and he meets his first person: a blue-skinned man who was a freak at the carnival that was included with the amusement park when Eddie was a kid. We already know enough about Eddie's life to know that this person was someone he only knew in passing. Yet, for some reason, this guy, not his brother or his mother, is the person who meets him first.

The blue gentleman fills Eddie in on the five-people thing, and they chat a bit. Then, casually, Eddie asks, *"How did you die?"*

"You killed me," the man says.

. . .

"You killed me." With those words, everything changes. It is like being electrified. This blue man who meant nothing, a stranger chosen at random, is suddenly inexorably tied into Eddie's life.

Eddie's second person is his captain from WWII. They talk; they go over many things: What a good soldier Eddie was; what happened when their band of brothers got captured; the horrible way they were treated by their captors; how they escaped; how they burned the bamboo buildings they left behind; and the moment when Eddie was shot in the leg—the injury that stole his future and ruined his life.

Finally, Eddie asks, *"Why you, Captain, why are you the one here to talk to me?"*

"Because I'm the one who shot you."

This is the one that really hits the viewer like a thunderbolt. (Probably the same thunderbolt that saved Luffy when he was about to be executed.) Suddenly, everything changed, everything about Eddie's life from that point on became different.

The captain goes on to explain why he did it. I will not tell you any more. If you have seen the movie, you know. If not, watch it!

Spoiler End

We could go on with *The Five People You Meet in Heaven*—there is a dramatic payload moment in at least four of the five sections—but that is enough to serve as an example.

Not every Payload moment has to involve *zings* and thunderbolts. But a good Payload moment will draw the reader deeper into the story. These are the moments when the purpose of the whole scene or story becomes clear, the moment that rewards the reader for the effort made so far.

Any time something supernatural happens, there should be a payload moment—otherwise, the supernatural becomes bland, like a travelogue. *"Today, we saw a giraffe, two aardvarks, and a phoenix. Ho hum."*

The supernatural—or wise or mysterious characters who might serve a similar purpose to the supernatural—should not come and go from the stage of your story without some kind of payload moment.

Bland

She walked down to the lake. The moon shone upon the water. It was a pleasant night.

Supernatural but still rather bland

She walked down to the lake. An angel stood upon the water. The angel smiled at her.

Payload Moment

She walked down to the lake. An angel stood upon the water. It said, "Your father is not dead."

The first two might be nice or beautiful or lyrical, but they don't propel the story forward. They don't grip the reader, and they don't reward the readers for the effort they put into reading thus far. The third one, on the other hand, provides a shiver-up-your-spine moment—a moment that rewards the reader for reading thus far and promises much more to come.

The moment in a mystery where you find out whodunit? That is a payload moment.

A payload moment propels the story forward and ties the scene into something greater... in relation to the plot or the universe itself... and it rewards the reader by saying, *"Something actually is going on in this story, and now you have been granted a glimpse of what that might be."*

A payload moment is both an answer to prior mysteries and a promise of wonders to come.

Exercise A: Payload *Zing*

Add a payload moment to your story.

Take a scene from your current work and add a payload moment, something that propels your story forward, adds a higher dimension, a new view of a character or a plot issue, or rewards the reader.

See if you can do this at least once for every short story and once per chapter—or in most chapters at least—for a novel.

Exercise B: Character Payload

Once you have done this for scenes, try it for characters. Can you tell your reader something new and revealing about your character that they did not previously know?

Something about his past that explains his present? Something that puts his behavior in a new light?

See if you can do that once for each character. (Donald Maass's character exercise discussed in Chapter Two is a great way to develop your character's payload moments.)

CHAPTER 14: THE TROUBLE WITH TROPES

Tropes: *Landmarks upon the landscape of the human heart.*

The Sliding Puzzle Map of Modern Tropes

During a trip my son and I took to Alaska, we visited a museum that had a gigantic map of Anchorage. This map was a dinner-table-sized version of those old-fashioned puzzles that used to come in Crackerjacks or with bubble gum, where you would slide square pieces around to form a picture.

Each block of this giant map in the Anchorage museum was a section of landscape: mountains, trees, roads, rivers, large bodies of water, etc. You could tell if the blocks had been arranged correctly by whether or not the pieces of landscape matched the blocks on all four sides. If a mountain fell off like a sheer wooden cliff, because the other half was missing, or if a winding river ended abruptly in blank green wood, you knew the blocks were in the wrong place.

Some errors, such as those mentioned above, were obvious. A moment's glance showed that half a mountain did not connect to the blue square representing the middle of the ocean. Other errors were more subtle. You had to study the map closely to notice that one black length of road had a different width from another, or that this section of green had a touch of blue at the corner that needed to be matched with a body of water.

Now you may be wondering what this has to do with… well, anything. Bear with me just a little longer.

The Landscape of the Human Heart

We think of stories as random collections of imaginary things that we can do anything with, but they are not. Stories have a logic to them that they must follow if they wish to entertain.

Stories horrify or delight—or whatever they set out to do—based on how well they recreate in our mind's eye the landscape of the human heart (or the soul or the psyche. Your pick.)

A writer's job is that of an adventurer. We gather our courage and set off to explore this landscape, seeking out portions of it yet unseen and returning to share our wondrous finds with our fellow human beings. We need to record what we find there faithfully. Otherwise, those who read our reports will know—in the same way that a person standing at the giant map and looking at the blocks can tell when they are out of place—that we have not done our work faithfully.

Now, what does this have to do with tropes?

A Turn of Tropes

Trope is derived from the Greek world *tropos*, which

means *turn*. Turn developed into the idea of style or manner, as in "a turn of phrase." Today, the word *trope* has come to mean "a figure of speech or a recurring theme," but once it had a more specific meaning.

Ruth Johnston, author of *All Things Medieval*, notes: *"During the time that church liturgy was in transition, churches began to expand the pure Bible material by inserting little expansion moments. The extra words or song was noted in the liturgy, and it's this they called the "trope."*

The first trope was in the Easter liturgy, when the angel at the empty tomb asks, 'Quem Quaeritis?' or 'Whom do you seek?'

"This was implied in the story, but no one gospel text had the full exchange,

'Whom do you seek?'

'Jesus of Nazareth.'

'Why seek ye the living among the dead? He is not here, he is risen. Go and tell the others.'

As the tenth and eleventh centuries progressed, more tropes were added, putting some narrative color into the Bible stories."

From this early history, tropes developed the more general meaning of a recurring theme. In particular, it came to rest in the critic's tool chest, of use to those comparing one story to another.

A Trope, Right, er, What Exactly Is That Again?

For some authors, tropes are a constant topic of discussion. For others, tropes have never come up. So let's take a moment to make certain that we are all on the same page. In modern usage, the term trope is used to mean "anything that is done regularly in stories."

Bad guys wearing black? Trope.

A prince rescuing a princess? Trope.

Superheroes wearing capes? Trope.

An old man sending a young one off on a quest? Trope.

Now, you may be asking: Is a trope a cliché? Not necessarily. The difference has been described as: A cliché is a trope that is not used well.

The Logic of Gravity

Imagine a river rushing down the high slopes of a mountain. Someone has plopped a huge boulder into the river's path. Where can the water go?

It could go left of the boulder. It could go to the right. It could work its way under the boulder. It could fill up a little pool until it flowed over the boulder. A ramp could be built so that the water flowed above the boulder and cascaded back to its riverbed in a waterfall.

All these things fall within the possibilities of what nature allows.

But the water cannot suddenly shoot upward or teleport to below the boulder or in other ways violate the laws of gravity.

If you were looking at this landscape and the water were following the laws of gravity, the mountainside would look correct to your eye. The peak of the mountain was up. The sides sloped down. The water ran the way your experience tells you water should run.

If this landscape were a story, each channel of water around the boulder would be a trope.

In some stories, when the water of the hero comes to the boulder of the obstacle, it goes left; in others, it goes right. In a mystery, the water might flow into an unexpected underground tunnel. In a romance, it might fill the pool formed behind the boulder slowly to flow over, the ensuing cascade forming a lovely picture.

In a spy thriller, the hero pushes a button and rides over the spout that suddenly shoots out of the hillside to redirect the water safely over the boulder. This kind of twist can be tricky to pull off, but if your hero is known by the reader to be the clever, gismo-using type, you can make it seem believable.

In each case, the flow of water, the plot and action of our story, has not violated the laws of nature or, in our case, the logic of the landscape of the human heart.

Tropes Gone Wrong

To return to our map analogy, imagine I took my waterfall block and stuck it randomly in the middle of the blue ocean block.

You would know instantly that something was off. This is not lifelike.

Because pieces of mountains, trees, waterfalls, and lakes cannot be placed randomly like Legos, stuck together in whatever order they happen to fall.

And yet, ladies and gentlemen, the modern use of tropes is often exactly like that.

The Horror That Is TV Tropes

I remember the day I first saw the website TV Tropes, which lists popular tropes from books and shows. Instantly my heart fell, because I was envisioning exactly what has come about today. Let me explain.

First, a disclaimer. There's absolutely nothing wrong with TV Tropes from a researcher's point of view. As a source of places that you can find certain ideas in stories, it is a fantastic resource, and I know that many fans have a great time with it. Nothing wrong with that!

It is only when authors begin taking it too seriously that it becomes a problem. Sadly, it has become a problem—or rather, the kind of thinking where *authors* analyses stories by tropes and then worry about them has become a problem.

A trope, as mentioned above, is a critic's tool. It is a way of looking at stories from the outside—as if the mountains and waterfalls and dells and parking lots of our landscape were independent Legos, and could all be examined individually. Specifically, it takes events that are natural elements of the landscape of the human psyche and treats them as if they are individual, unrelated elements that can be manipulated independently, much like thinking that you could place a waterfall without any high source of water nearby for it to be falling from.

Tropes are *not* a writer's tool. In fact, from the writer's point of view, there is no such thing as a trope—and herein we discover our problem. As I mentioned, the moment I realized that someone was codifying the turns of stories and labeling them, I knew what the response would be.

Authors, who are not the most confident of folk in creation, would become self-conscious.

They would begin to hesitate to report faithfully upon the findings of their explorations of the landscape of the soul for fear of describing something that would superficially sound too much like someone else's report.

I expected this, particularly of newer writers, still learning the craft. I just never imagined that one of the first to fall would be Disney.

I love the older Disney cartoons, the ones based on fairy-tales. Their storytelling is fantastic. In the more recent Disney movies, however, the scriptwriters have been so self-conscious of the tropes in their cartoons that people enjoy poking fun at on the internet that they have begun ruining their own stories. They "reverse" tropes for no reason, not by coming up with a clever new way for the water to get by the boulder, but by having it fly upward, for no reason at right angles to—well, everything—so as to hit the viewer in the eye.

And when they don't do this, they add cringeworthy dialogue to try and explain away tropes—pulling the viewer from the story and entirely sapping the power of the turn of the story they are mistakenly calling a trope.

All of which have made some of their more recent films much less enjoyable.

Disney is by far not the only one doing this, but they are the most prominent. All this is the result of self-consciousness, of authors who are too embarrassed to report what they have discovered in their imaginary travels, because they have been cowed by those who believe that stories should be reduced to a pile of tropes and then judged on whether or not those tropes are new.

They act as if the features of the imaginary landscape could be combined in arbitrary combinations, so that mountains stuck out sideways from waterfalls and oceans flopped around in mid-air, unsupported by bedrock or solid land. As if majestic mountains and babbling brooks and cascading waterfalls and foggy dells are all old hat, and only stories that invent new landscape features no one has ever seen before are worth anyone's time.

Can you imagine holding a world-traveler to this standard: "Oh, we don't want to hear about mountains that are even higher than the Alps and produce pink salt! Give us a terrain feature that has never been seen before!"

People who talk about tropes in this manner betray themselves. The true explorers of the imaginary kingdom—whether authors or readers—instantly recognize them for what they are: posers who have never traveled through the landscape of the soul—posers like someone who claimed to be a world traveler but who got all their fantastic stories from travelogues, second hand, having never looked upon the wonders with their own eyes.

Trick and Consequence

All this brings us to the most important question: *What exactly is a story?* What is this landscape that dwells within the human heart?

It is the consequences of The Trick.

As we discussed in Chapter One, The Trick is the primary principle of storytelling, how stories come alive through contrast, how a scene needs to end in a different place from where it starts. The Trick is a phenomenon that draws the attention of human beings—i.e., a feature of our mental landscape. It is *not* something we pull out of our pocket when writing by the seat of our pants. Or, specifically, it is *not* arbitrary.

We don't get to invent the features of the landscape of the human heart; we don't get to decide what human nature finds compelling.

We only get to arrange the elements in new and pleasing patterns, like a landscaper who has to work with the same rock and flowers and woodchips and grass as other landscapers, but who, nonetheless, can design a yard that looks like no other.

. . .

Going Down to Go Up

The Trick says that if you want a happy end to your scene, you have to start off sad (or tired or grumpy or angry, etc.) If you want to go up, you have to first go down. This is because something that starts in a "down" position has farther to go to reach an "up" position than something which was already near the top, so it gives an impression of greater achievement.

The landscapes of the human heart that storytelling explores follow the Trick, because starting-down-to-go-up being more dramatic than starting-up-to-go-up is how the human heart is formed, the same way that real landscapes are constrained by elements such as gravity.

If a boy is going to go on adventure, it is more startling if he is a small, poor boy with little worldly support than if he is a well-to-do boy with all that the world can offer.

If he is going to fight a monster, it is more dramatic if it is a gigantic dragon who is going to eat his village if he fails than if it is an overweight hog who could probably be chased away by yelling and waving one's arms.

If he is going to rescue a girl, it is more compelling if she is a princess and the future of the kingdom is at stake than if she is the baker's assistant whom no one will really miss.

These things are not true because of custom or "the Patriarchy" or culture. They are not true because someone stole the right trope.

They are true because they are true.

They are true because the landscape of the human heart is an objective place, in the sense that its rules are not arbitrary. A princess, who represents the love and fears of a nation, is objectively more dramatic than a random person who has no particular ties.

Not because of classism or feminism or any ism, but because people who have more effect on the world around them (as in, a person who is the daughter of the ruler of that place) have more potential for drama—more ability to go up or down, to end happily or sadly—than someone who has less effect on the world within the story.

The Wonder of the Wood Perilous

If you want to understand the principles of storytelling—the basic features of the landscape of the human heart, you could not do better than to read fairytales. Some might say that fairytales are pure trope, but it would be more accurate to say: *Fairytales are pure Trick.*

A tailor's son must face a giant. A poor youngest son must make a sad princess smile, or he will die. A goose girl must win the heart of a prince.

The lowest are exalted. The mighty fall.

Good stories do not follow the "tropes" of fairytales because they are unimaginative, uncreative. They follow familiar same patterns because that is what the landscape of the heart looks like.

Tired Tropes

That is not to say that tired tropes don't exist.

There was a reason that I used water running through a channel for my analogy. Stories are like water cutting a channel through the countryside. At first, they are fresh, sprightly steams, and they burble over the rocks. With time, they develop into quiet meandering rivers that wander aimlessly across the plains. When this happens, an opportunity arises for a twist—a creative and unexpected new direction for the water of our story to flow. It is a bit like cutting a new channel so that water no longer has to flow through the ox-bow of a meander. At such times, turning a previous trope—a well-followed path, or an ox-bow if you prefer—on its head sometimes works splendidly.

It is fresh and unexpected. Readers love it.

But it is not arbitrary. It still has to follow the logic of the laws of the landscape, or the excitement will be like a lightning bolt. There one moment and then forgotten. If the twist is dramatic purely because of shock value, it will only work once or twice.

A waterfall in the middle of an ocean might be made to seem reasonable in one story, but it would be hard to pull it off again and again. As soon as the shock is over, the reversal fails to continue to entertain.

An Example

A good example of a reversal is the movie *Shrek*. (Spoiler warning for *Shrek*) The princess is under a curse. She is in danger of turning into an ogress. We all expect a knight to save her and help her remain human. Instead, she chooses her cursed state so as to find love with a gruff but loveable ogre.

Unexpected, yet amusing.

And it followed logically from the set-up: Girl has ogre curse, ogre is love interest.

However, since *Skrek*, other stories have tried to follow this same pattern. They do not gain anything from freshness, because it has been done before. And "girl chooses not to be human rather than to be cured" is like the waterfall in the middle of the ocean. It has to be handled expertly—with one of those transparent pipes you see for such things at fairs—or it begins to lead to unpleasant places, to go against the flow of the rivers that run through the landscape of the heart.

And readers balk.

Dangerous Territory

One of the dangers of "reversing expectations" as the term is often used nowadays—of going against a trope just to go against it—is that the story may fall into wish-fulfillment territory.

The idea "an orphan who has a hard life persevering and making good" has proper application of the Trick both emotionally and practically. The reader believes that the prize was fairly bought through the character's struggle and suffering. But if a character makes good without any price attached—that is wish-fulfillment and, frankly, not very interesting to read.

When the character is a girl, she is often called a MarySue.*

Wish-fulfillment stories are often boring or worse, because the lack of struggle makes the character's success unbelievable instead of satisfying.

---

*—The term MarySue comes from a Star Trek fan fic parody, in which the author, in order to mock the wish-fulfillment aspect of many pieces of fan fiction, had her character Crewman MarySue be good at everything and adored by all the main characters on the Enterprise.

. . .

Atlas to the Imaginary Country

Which leads us to the most important question of all: *Where is this landscape of the heart, and how do we get there?* How do we learn to see it? How do we develop the courage to explore its wilderness, the eye to see its mountains and valleys, the skill to come back from these far places and report truly upon what we have seen? How do we learn to allow our stories to follow the lay of this land, so that our readers feel in their hearts that what we are reporting is faithful and true?

How do we put aside concerns of originality and "whether this trope has been used before" and write the best story we can write?

Farther Up and Farther In

The answer is both simple and difficult: *By going there.*

By daydreaming.

If you lay back and imagine your story, if you let your mind go and move beyond what you have already invented, you can reach a point where you begin to ask the question: How can I make this more...?

Where the "..." that you want more of is whatever quality your story represents.

Let us use a well-known example. I want to write a story about someone who faces down a great evil. Hmm...

Wouldn't it be more dramatic if he were a boy rather than a man? A boy who has less freedom, less innate strength facing off against danger is more dramatic than someone with more ability.

How about if he were an orphan? Isn't that even more

dramatic? An orphan boy who doesn't even have parents facing off against this terrible evil?

But what if he wasn't just an orphan, he's an orphan being raised by people who don't like him. They dislike him so much, they make him sleep in a cupboard under the stairs.

Not only is he parentless and disliked—living in a cupboard under the stairs no less!—but he's famous. And because he's famous, other kids automatically dislike him, because they are jealous, and it never occurs to them that his life might be so awful.

And what if...

You get the picture. Hopefully, you see how by making Harry Potter's lows even lower it paves the way for his heights to be even higher.

Now, it's your turn...

Exercise A: Exploring the Landscape of the Heart

The best way to learn about the imaginary country is to explore it. How do we do that? By going there. Specifically, by daydreaming about pushing the limits of the story's current situations.

Take an aspect of your story: a dramatic scene, the background of your character, an aspect of your plot.

Daydream. What could you do differently? What could you do to make the heights higher and the depths lower? To make the whole thing more iconic? More compelling? Sadder? Happier? (Yes, this is similar to the Plot We've Got exercise, but here it doesn't have to be just plot twits. It can be backstory as well.)

How can you provide more torque on your characters to

put them under greater pressure and make their experience more epic?

Without any concern for what you are actually willing to use in your story, make a list of things that could increase the drama, sadness, happiness—whatever quality you wish to increase.

1) Make a list of things that follow logically from your premise that might do this.

2) Make a second list of things that do not follow—things that wouldn't work for your story. Notice how the story feels flatter, more like fan fiction, if you indulge in these more unrealistic directions.

Take at least one item from each list and explain why it works or does not work.

Example:

For Part 1) You decide to twist the knife, making the life of your character, Harry Potter, more painful. He discovers he isn't actually without family after all. He has a godfather —who is thought by everyone in the world to be a horrendous criminal, so he can't live with him or really benefit from his existence.

This makes his life harder because now he has the promise of a real life with someone who loves him, but unfair misunderstandings are standing in his way—making his loneliness even more poignant.

. . .

For Part 2) Your character, Harry Potter, is a chick magnet with a girl on either arm. All the girls adore him. Also, whenever a professor is uppity to him, he gets petty revenge on the teacher, showing the person up in front of everyone for a good laugh.

Both of these things decrease Harry's alienation and misery, making his life easier and the drama of his situation less.

Being a chick magnet would make his character both less lonely and more shallow. Getting revenge on the professors who mistreat or belittle him would, again, decrease his alienation and misery, reducing the drama of his situation.

Exercise B: Rescuing Reversed Expectations

Take the version of your character from Exercise A, Part 2 or invent another character for this exercise. Give the character a handful of qualities that do not immediately draw sympathy: rich, successful, snide, uncaring, petty, etc.

How would you make this character appealing to a reader? How would you make a story about this character not merely wish-fulfillment? What would you have to change about the story premise? What kind of problems would you have to add to help the reader engage with such a character?

Examples:
1) A character with a big family is not as sympathetic, right off the bat, as an orphan, but maybe he is the odd

person out in his family? Or maybe his family is big and loving, but this causes its own problems as the character is always being sucked into the dramas of the other family members.

2) A snide, uncaring character can be great fun, Jack Vance's Cugel the Clever or Harry Flashman from *The Flashman Papers* can be great fun. They do take petty revenge and sometimes have a girl on each arm, but, intriguingly, they often don't succeed. They are clever and tricky and come out on top in many ways, but often, they fail at whatever it was they were actually hoping to achieve.

3) A favorite conversation in our family is "How would you improve *Boruto*?"

Naruto is a Japanese anime about a young man who starts downtrodden and disliked, with nothing, and grows to be a great man. *Boruto* is a story about his son. Only the son has none of the qualities that made his father so likable. He is not alone, not downtrodden, etc., and his father is a very powerful hero. Worse, Boruto starts his show disliking his father—the character the viewers like the most.

With so much against Boruto, how would one make a story about the son of a powerful successful man work? (We usually drop the dislike of his father first thing and go from there.)

Pick some unappealing qualities of your own and give it a shot!

Bonus:

If, in the previous exercise, you come up with an idea that is better than one in your Work In Progess, write a scene where you introduce the new idea.

(Example. If your character, Harold Potter, was an orphan, but now you suddenly decide you are going to call him Harry and make his life so much more miserable by banishing him to live in a cupboard, write the scene where you introduce the idea that he lives in a cupboard. Etc.)

FINAL WORD: WRITING TIPS

And so we come to the end of our journey together.

I wish to take a moment to explain how this book came to be. Many years ago, I began to pray that I would be able to better understand the writing process. I didn't just want to write better (my literary efforts were rather abysmal back then,) I wanted to understand why better was better.

What was it that made the great works great?

For many years, these prayers had no answer. I struggled with stories that glittered in my mind but lay dully upon the page. Then, slowly, came glimmers of light. My husband, author John C. Wright, and I figured out *The Trick* and *Two Strings*. I discovered Donald Maass's book. That was a big step!

Not wanting to forget what I was learning, I began to note down the things I had figured out as writing tips for myself. Once in a while, I would mention this list to other authors who would ask to see it. To my surprise, again and again, they mentioned how helpful my tips were.

In 2009, I launched a blog called Wrights' Writing Corner (originally my husband and I were both writing for this blog, hence the name) and began writing posts about writing. I posted my Writing Tips. Then, I began writing an article for each of the Writing Tips. Much of this book was born in these Writing Tip articles. The brief descriptions of each concept at the beginning of the chapters come, for the most part, from my original Writing Tip sheet.

My hope for you, dear students, is that you will begin to keep your own Writing Tips sheets. When you grasp something new, when you suddenly see how to accomplish something you had not understood before, jot down a note.

This way, you, too, will be able to remember what you learned later.

Then, when you write, glance over the list of tips to see if you have forgotten something that perhaps should go into your manuscript. (You would be amazed at the number of times I have finished a work and glanced at my Writing Tips, only to discover that I had left out something crucial—such as sense impressions in a description.)

To help you along, here is the short version of what we have covered. You can adapt any of them that have sparked useful ideas to your own list or just glance at this one occasionally to jog your memory.

Writing Tips from the Art and Craft of Writing

The Trick: *If you want a scene to lead to an emotional reaction, start with the opposite reaction.*

Living Characters: *To make a character come to life, give him two conflicting qualities or goals.*

Descriptions That Grip: *Add two to five senses to every description.*

Two Strings: *Two separate issues need to be going in each scene.*

Anticipation: *The secret to engaging readers is: If the character cares, the reader cares.*

The Ultimate Secret: *The secret to making every story—and scene— engaging and satisfying is to give the reader a glimpse of the character's purpose.*

Open with a Hook: *The best way to hook the reader is to leave him with a question that is not answered until deep into the work.*

Open active: *Start the scenes with changes underway and then explain how you got there... unless the changes are significant.*

Plot: *Ask yourself: How can I make this more...?*

Inserting Information: *Backstory that the reader longs for becomes revelation.*

Satisfying Endings: *Tie the beginning and the end together —balance satisfaction and surprise.*

Conveying Emotion: *Add visceral reactions—physical involuntary reactions—to heighten the connection with the reader.*

Interior Dialogue: *Readers don't trust dialogue. Let your characters think, and let what they think be juxtaposed to the dialogue, showing the readers a new angle.*

Payload Moments: *Every scene should have a moment that moves the plot along or heightens awareness, drawing the reader into something greater.*

Tropes: *Landmarks upon the landscape of the human heart.*

In Conclusion

When we set out to write stories, we wish to share the visions that have come into our minds and touched our hearts. We wish to share them in such a way that they will touch the hearts of others—or scare them, or make them laugh, or whatever it is that we wish to express.

The more people appreciate a given story—the more they interact with it or refer to it—the more real it becomes. Some stories have gained so much reality that they have taken on a life of their own. Some have even delighted hearts for more than three thousand years.

When we write, we set out to enter this parade of lasting tales that has been going since before recorded history. Whether our place in this parade is large or small may be out of our control, but nothing can stop us from joining!

So on those dark days, when the words won't flow, and it seems your efforts will never be repaid, don't give up!

Don't listen to the voice of hopelessness, the whisper of despair, the snide snicker of, "Be practical, man. You can't write." Because while many forces in the world might keep you from some particular measurement of success, the only thing that can keep you from writing is: *if you stop writing.*

Nothing else can stop you!

And with this, we conclude our time together.

God willing, something in these lessons will stick, allowing you to better convey to the page the story that shines in your mind. Then those who read your works will find them to be anything but *mere words on a page.*

RESOURCES

Donald Maass – New York agent
  Writing the Breakout Novel and *Writing the Breakout Novel Workbook*

Margie Lawson – therapist and teacher of writing
  https://www.margielawson.com/

Allen L. Wold – science fiction author
  http://allen-wold.com/

Long Live the Queen - Video game
  Long Live the Queen by Hanako: https://www.hanakogames.com/llq.shtml
  Or on Steam: https://store.steampowered.com/app/251990/Long_Live_The_Queen/

Other works by L. Jagi Lamplighter:
  http://www.ljagilamplighter.com/works/

Where to find *The Art and Craft of Writing* videos:
http://www.superversivesf.com/?page_id=1737

To inquire about online interactive writing classes:
arhyalon@gmail.com

ACKNOWLEDGMENTS

I would like to thank:

The Backers of The Art and Craft of Writing Indiegogo Campaign, who made this book and the related video series possible.

Ken Dickeson, our narrator and Ben Zwycky, our videographer. Ken's amazing voice work and Ben's inspired images have brought this course to life.

Shana Bucks for her help recording my portion of the course.

Jason Rennie of Superversive Press, for expressing a willingness to take a chance on us.

Kevin Ward for his proofreading.

The many students who have taken the class and helped me discover ideas that were unclear and how better to present them.

And, most of all, the students of the original Guinea Pig The Art and Craft of Writing Class: Ben Wheeler, Marina Fontaine, Corey McCleary, Frank Luke, Kristi Hawes, Christi Whitehead, Rylee Barfield, Charles Perez, Robert Dean, Nancy Vest, Shelley Stewart, Karl Gallagher, Denton Salle,

Paul Piatt, Hans Schantz, Sam Robb, Kristine Keller, Sandra Bell, Gina Westenberg, Anja Westernberg, Alex Edwards, Erin Furby, Devin Malcolm Robertson, Marilyn Robertson, Sue Freivald, Paul Go, Dorothy Grant, Margot St. Aubin, Christopher R. DiNote, James Pyles, Nathan Parrello, Monica Celio, and Christine Chase.

And the first three, who dared it even before the Guinea Pigs: Orville Wright, Juss Wright, and A. M. Freeman.

www.ingramcontent.com/pod-product-compliance
Lightning Source LLC
LaVergne TN
LVHW041219080426
835508LV00011B/995